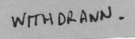

BEYOND THE LOOKING GLASS

BEYOND THE LOOKING GLASS

Overcoming the Seductive Culture of Corporate Narcissism

Alan Downs

AMACOM

American Management Association

New York • Atlanta • Boston • Chicago • Kansas City • San Francisco • Washington, D.C.
Brussels • Mexico City • Tokyo • Toronto

This publication is designed to provide accurate and authoritative
information in regard to the subject matter covered. It is sold with
the understanding that the publisher is not engaged in rendering
legal, accounting, or other professional service. If legal advice or
other expert assistance is required, the services of a competent professional person should be sought.

Library of Congress Cataloging-in-Publication Data

Downs, Alan.
    Beyond the looking glass : overcoming the seductive culture of corporate
narcissism / Alan Downs.
        p.   cm.
    Includes bibliographical references and index.
    ISBN 0-8144-0343-3
    1. Industrial management—United States.   2. Profit.
3. Narcissism.   I. Title.
HD70.U5D68   1997
658—dc21   96-52475
                                                               CIP

Printing Number

10   9   8   7   6   5   4   3   2   1

To
Kevin Sloan

Contents

Preface   ix

Introduction: Battling for the Soul of Corporate
           America   1

Section 1:   **The Corporate Narcissist**   9

One   Image Is All That Matters   11
Two   Building the Empire: Management
             Style of a Narcissist   31

Section 2:   **Narcissism in the Organization**   75

Three   The Narcissistic Organization   77
Four   Where Winning Is All That Matters   91
Five   Profit and the Dark Side   111
Six   Corporate Evangelists and Chronic
             Campaigns   127

Section 3:   **Beyond Narcissism**   137

Seven   The Organization as Reluctant Host   139
Eight   How to Work in the Narcissistic
             Organization   161

Nine   A Second-Helping of Success   177
Ten   Looking at Ourselves   193

Epilogue: Reversing the Flow   203

Notes   211

Index   215

Preface

The last quarter-century has brought pandemic change to corporate America. As the twentieth century draws to a close, the grand old institutions of commerce are being transformed at a speed and degree never before seen. Ostensibly made to solve fundamental and persistent problems, these changes have failed to produce their guarantee: a more efficient and productive enterprise. The sad truth is that many corporations are limping into the millennium with a dazzling facelift and a morbid prognosis.

Inside the corporation, life has never been more stifling, and, some would even say, downright miserable. The recent changes have robbed the company man of his treasures. Job security is gone. Upward mobility has become a lateral move. Pay raises have become an acute disappointment. And worst by far is the threefold loss of job satisfaction, the fulfillment of ongoing work relationships, and the love of a job well done. All of these have been painfully torn from the hands of the corporate citizen.

The perpetrators of this violence to the corporate soul are an expanding group of managers whose only operating value is self-interest. They entered the corporate arena with a burning need to prove their worthiness and a shocking lack of empathy for those whom they manipulate for their own benefit. They are narcissists who have come to power within the corporation.

These narcissistic managers have contaminated many a corporate culture with their nihilistic ways. While they mouth the rhetoric of organization values and mission, in practice they reject all but what will suit their self-serving goals. They forsake content and meaning for an image of success. Winning, whatever the cost, is all that matters.

The spread of narcissistic management is slowly darkening the corporate landscape. Executive by executive, department by department, it comes; a division here, a subsidiary there, until ultimately the entire organization succumbs.

The narcissists arrive with a highly seductive and simplistic message on their lips. Profit, they say, is the only true measure of corporate success. Increase profit and you increase the strength and viability of the corporation. To the rank-and-file they say: Enhance my career and you increase your own job security and wealth.

But the narcissists are dead wrong. Their obsession with profit is merely an extension of their own obsession with a grand image of success. The economic returns of a corporation extend far beyond the mere dollars returned to investors and senior managers. The corporation is a multifaceted anchor of economic stability that extends to the livelihood of employees and the strength of the community. Profit must be celebrated, but it can never be separated from the broader context of all corporate stakeholders. To do so is to reduce the corporation to little more than a tool for greed.

In this book, I chronicle the path of narcissism in the organization. Drawing on my own training in psychology and experience as a management consultant, I compare the psychological dysfunction of narcissism and the behavior of many corporate managers. The result is a shocking, perhaps even harrowing picture of the corporate narcissist. Throughout the book, I give numerous real life examples of executives whose self-serving behavior is classic narcissism.

Beginning at its roots in the lives and careers of aspiring narcissists, I describe how it innocently grows from energetic overachievement into manipulative self-enhancement. The narcissist hungers for power and recognition, hiding a highly personal quest behind a smoke screen of corporate objectives. He shackles his employees with the yoke of a supporting and powerless role.

As narcissism grows, it recomposes the organization into a magnet that attracts other narcissists and convinces the remaining employees to play by strict narcissistic rules. In time, all meaning and passion within the organization is transformed into a hollow facade, and corporate mission becomes nothing more than a punch line for an advertising campaign, with little meaning beyond luring potential customers and investors.

In the last section of the book, I take a look at companies that have consistently resisted the corporate culture of narcissism. I show how it is possible to succeed in business by enhancing the collective good of customers, employees, managers, and investors. The hallmarks of these companies are always honesty, honored commitments, and a passion for the corporate mission. In return, employees respond with loyalty, personal sacrifice, and protective care of the organization. Ultimately, these are the companies that fulfill the corporate obligation to society and the economy.

I have used a few necessary conventions in writing this book. First, you will also notice that when referring to both genders, I often defaulted to the male pronoun. This is merely a literary convenience and should in no way imply that narcissism is the sole property of the male gender. The condition is, in fact, gender independent.

Secondly, throughout the book are numerous examples of narcissistic management behavior. Because of the obvious sensitivity around this issue, I have disguised many of these individuals, changing their names and situations. While protecting them, I have tried to remain true to the relevant facts of each scenario. In every instance where a company is called by name, those facts are presented without changes.

Finally, I owe an enormous intellectual debt to Alice Miller, whose writings[1] on the topic of narcissism enlightened and enraged but have continued for more than a decade to teach me. She, more than any other, opened my eyes to the pain and destruction of narcissism. If ever I have been permitted to stand on the mountain and view the path beyond narcissism, it is because she generously permitted me and many others to do so on the shoulders of her brave and loving words.

BEYOND THE LOOKING GLASS

Introduction

Battling for the Soul of Corporate America

A rumbling is coming from just over the horizon. The sound is a heated battle for the soul of corporate America. The rumblings of war explode in sound bites that ring from the covers of *Newsweek, Fortune,* and *Time.* Their headlines document the battles over repeated corporate mergers, soaring executive pay, stagnant wages for most employees, and unprecedented layoffs. Even *The New York Times* has documented this war, giving its coverage of layoff casualties more continuous space than any other story since the infamous Pentagon Papers were published.

The entire corporate world shudders as the valueless management philosophy of a few powerful executives infiltrates company after company, leaving behind hollow corpses of a bygone era. These executives arrive under the guise of cost-cutting and leave with their pockets full of bounty. These are the corporate narcissists.

The tools of total quality and reengineering are no impediment to these aggressive warriors, who are absolutely determined to raise profits by cutting costs, and to cut until it hurts. Cut until no visible sign of the problem is left. Cut until

Wall Street applauds. Cut until their paychecks exceed their own insatiable greed.

The cries of the opposition only inspire their indignation. These opposing voices, they say, are nothing more than a sure sign that corporate parentalism—or, as they call it, socialism—has persisted too long and whetted the laborer's appetite for entitlement and laziness. In the words of Cypress Semiconductor CEO T. J. Rodgers, society has no claim to a job that "has no right to exist."

To the corporate narcissist, the universe revolves around one thing: profit. Forget social responsibility. Forget caring for employees. Forget the environment. Condemn whatever and whoever stands between you and profit. That, the narcissists, proudly proclaim (and the media so often echoes) is the Ultimate Corporate Mandate.

Should one dispute this revered commandment, the narcissists are quick to threaten the loss of jobs. "Jobs!" they cry. "Remember your jobs! Do you want to work? Do you want your neighbors to work? Do you want your community to thrive? Then do as we say or your risk a jobless damnation."

THE PURISTS VS. THE STAKEHOLDERS

The war rages on. On one side are the shareholder-purists who hold the narcissistic belief that the *sole* purpose of the corporation is to provide themselves with a return on investment. On the opposing side are those who require that the corporation be a broader servant of society, providing direct benefit to "stakeholders" (employees, suppliers, management, customers, community, and, yes, shareholders). The tug-of-war between these two groups has surged across most of this century, but recently it has developed into a polarizing and militant war. Both sides of the war are firmly entrenched in ideology.

At the very center of this controversy lies corporate mission—the value of an organization to society. One side, the shareholder-purists, proclaim that the only mission of an organization is to pay investors a return on investment. By evoking the theories of supply-side and "trickle-down" economics, they hold that returns paid to investors will inevitably benefit all of society. On the other side, the stakeholders claim that the corporation must serve the best interests of those who actually do the work (employees) and others who support the existence of the corporation (suppliers and the community). For stakeholders, the concept of profit is much broader than a dividend; it is a benefit that is shared with all who are part of the corporation.

The shareholder-purists laugh at the diverse goals of the stakeholders. In the words of one of the more vocal purists, Albert Dunlap, CEO of Sunbeam, "Stakeholders are total rubbish. It's the shareholders who own the company. Not enough American executives care about the shareholders."[1] Master lexicologist and nationally syndicated columnist William Safire pushes the envelope even further by equating the philosophy of the stakeholders to socialism. "Enter the New Socialist Person. He or she is called the 'stakeholder.' Remember that word; it has replaced 'proletariat' in the lexicon of the left."[2]

In the Beginning: The Corporation

While each side is busily decrying the other as un-American, it is the stakeholder argument that has its roots firmly planted in the history of the American corporation. Simply put, the corporation was originally invented as a means to serve the public interest, not as a vehicle for profit. Profit did not surface as the primary corporate motive until the nineteenth century, nearly two hundred years later.

The construct of the "corporation" was invented to fulfill functions for which the government was unequipped. The very first corporations on North American shores were organized to explore and settle the New World. Companies like the Massachusetts Bay Company and the Plymouth Company were organized and chartered by the government of England to settle and develop the colonies. These corporate charters were granted for a specific purpose and time. Once fulfilled, the charter was revoked and the corporation dissolved.

During the eighteenth and nineteenth centuries, many, including top political leaders, viewed corporations as dangerous entities. These were creatures "without conscience or soul," and consequently, they required certain restrictions. Among the legal limits placed on corporate charters were time limits (usually twenty years) and a specific public objective to uphold. In addition, the stockholders of the company were fully liable for all corporate debts.[3]

The role of the corporation began to change during the mid-1800s. During this time, many fledgling states tried to attract settlers. These states quickly discovered that by lowering restrictions on corporations, they could attract new businesses and the accompanying employees. By 1875, many states were in a heated race to become the most corporate-friendly. Eventually, Delaware won the race by dropping virtually all legal limits on incorporation, including an elimination of corporate taxation.

During the late 1800s public service took a backseat to profit as the primary goal of the corporation. In the years following the Civil War, giant corporate empires were born and run by men like Cornelius Vanderbilt, Andrew Carnegie, and J. Pierpont Morgan. As Matthew Josephson's book *The Robber Barons* chronicles, with few legal limitations to hold him back, this new breed of corporate tycoon unscrupulously plundered the American marketplace and exploited workers. By the early twentieth century, these corporations had amassed such wealth and power that popular opinion turned against them and ushered in the trust-busting era of Teddy Roosevelt.

The robber barons of the early twentieth century were among the first shareholder-purists. They believed in pursuing profit at all cost. Profit, they believed, was justification for exploiting workers, devastating communities, and consuming large shares of the earth's natural resources. Profit could rationalize anything.[4]

This single-minded purist camp was dealt a severe blow when the stock market collapsed in 1929. Suddenly, millions of Americans were bankrupt and out of work. Corporations could not afford to ignore their workers or the communities in which they existed. Workers were customers, as Henry Ford so aptly discovered, and if they didn't earn a livable wage, they could not buy goods and services. Consequently, many companies turned their attention to improving the economic status of the stakeholders.

THE CURRENT CONFLICT

From World War II until the present, purists and stakeholders have been slugging it out in the boardroom and in the legislative arena. Purists choose the more traditional weapons of legislative lobbying and influence-peddling, while stakeholders use the grassroots-guerrilla tactics of marches, pickets, boycotts, and voting. Each side works furiously to undo the latest victory of its opponent.

In years past this conflict was between labor and management, but no more. Sympathizers to both sides can be found at all levels within the corporation and within all economic strata of the community. The fight is not just for wages, benefits or retirement; it is a battle over the very purpose of the corporation.

THE PURIST REVIVAL

Since the mid-1970s, the purist camp has seen considerable growth. Those who elevate profit above all other considerations have declared war on corporate purpose. With steely determination, they strip the organization of everything that doesn't directly and immediately contribute to profit— everything, that is, but their own paychecks. Those have risen dramatically year after year.

In the decade of the 1980s, society watched with pleasure and then fear as the purists slashed and plundered company after company. As the go-go decade progressed, the promise of "wealth for all" turned into blatant greed as the entire savings and loan industry became a symbol of what could happen if the hunger for profit went unchecked. Big, short-term pay-outs became extended nightmares as a few self-serving businessmen dipped into the coffers of society to fill their own bank accounts.

Historians and social critics labeled the 1980s the decade of greed, suggesting that indulgent practices ended with the decade. But as the nineties have progressed, little has changed. The actors and the set of the eighties' drama may have changed, but in the nineties, the plot remains the same.

Close examination of this greed shows that it is something more than just an insatiable hunger for profit. The profit obsession, as it turns out, is but a symptom of a far more disturbing and resilient problem. Along with the greed has come a marked loss of corporate meaning. Corporations that once claimed a specific mission have become monolithic shells that have been stripped of their commitments to customers, employees, and communities. Examples abound of companies that have abandoned communities after decades of residence, laid off employees approaching retirement, and terminated services to long-term customers (e.g., insurance company withdrawals from Florida after Hurricane Andrew), all in the pursuit of higher profits. Some of these companies have even been willing to jeopardize the safety and well-being of their customers to save an extra buck or two (e.g., the auto industry's reluctance to include airbags prior to federal regulations requiring them to do so).

With this loss of corporate values, the profile of the successful manager has also changed. The corporate hero is no longer the manager who successfully balances the demands of management, customers, and employees. The new supermanager is a strident athlete-warrior whose focus on results is at the detriment of process. Sadly, to be consumed with one's own career is now acceptable, provided that one's immediate financial results are equivalent to the size of one's ego.

THE PURIST AS NARCISSIST

This is more than mere lust for profit; it is narcissism. The world of the narcissist is characterized by a dearth of values, a carefully crafted image, an absence of empathy or any deep emotion, and an obsession with personal gain. What better describes many of today's corporations?

In these companies, values statements are carefully worded and quickly discarded. Wrongdoing is defined not by respected ethics, but by the size of the legal liability. Emotion as expressed in loyalty to employees, caring for customers, or altruistic philanthropy in the community is considered a management weakness.

Narcissism as a corporate expression starts as an individual experience. As a few narcissistic managers gain a foothold, they slowly begin to spread their dogma throughout the organization. With time and success, they may even succeed in dominating the corporate culture, forcing everyone to play by their rules. Even those who disdain their methods must engage in the kill-or-be-killed competition.

To understand the culture of the corporate narcissism, we must look at the source of the malady: the individual narcissist. The narcissist turned corporate citizen is the root of the larger movement that is sweeping American business and threatening to kill the corporate soul.

Section 1

THE CORPORATE NARCISSIST

ONE

Image Is All That Matters

The modern corporation is plagued by a disease that is spreading with epidemic proportions throughout the business world. Many unsuspecting corporations are falling prey to the ravages of this silent killer, which destroys the organization from the inside out. Once the corrosive plague runs its course, all that is left is a hollow shell of what was before.

The disease is *corporate narcissism*.

Corporate narcissism is a deceptive killer. First it attacks a few key management positions; then, if allowed to flourish, it spreads quickly throughout the organization. When the disease first appears, it looks deceptively enticing: It starts with the ambitious new manager who is willing to do whatever he can to get ahead. He has a hard-driving style that is strictly results-oriented. His actions are always in his own best interest. And very often, he succeeds.

Others in the organization take note of his success. They learn the new law of corporate warfare: Attack or be attacked. Look out for yourself because no one else will. Use whatever or whomever you need to get ahead. Always make sure you come out on top and looking good.

Before long, this way of thinking and operating spreads. The organization becomes a loose federation of corporate bandits who pretend to be loyal to the whole but, in truth, are only faithful to themselves. When forced to choose between the collective good and their own self-interest, the latter always prevails.

This creates a cutthroat organization that wastes vast resources on competing with itself. Managers feigning loyalty to the team silently plot against one another and build "empires" to maintain their hierarchical power. In the process, dedicated and talented employees become expendable pawns in political battles and territorial squabbles. Those who survive are not the best, but the most politically adept.

Once corporate narcissism has run its course, the organization becomes a rigid facade. Ensconced in hard-won positions of power, managers recite the latest corporate catchphrases, but resist any change that reduces their dominion. Everything—customers, employees, products, communities, suppliers—is expendable to the power of the narcissistic organization.

WHAT IS NARCISSISM?

Narcissism is certainly not unique to the business world. The word *narcissism* was borrowed from mythology and over centuries of usage has grown far beyond its original meaning. Like a well-worn coin, the term has been traded about by literary writers, mythologists, psychologists, sociologists, theologians, and armchair philosophers of all professions, wearing down the coin's imprint but never its value. Each has taken the word to describe a uniquely human experience which, despite its commonness in modern society, is difficult to describe. Hence, the word has acquired a fuzzy but unmistakably dark reputation.

The concept of narcissism is one of those natural paradoxes: a simple idea that is deceivingly complex. At first glance, the word appears to describe the person who is utterly in love with himself, whose self-confidence knows no limits, and whose morals are strictly hedonistic. Beneath the surface, however, narcissism is something very different.

Story of Narcissus

To understand this complex idea, it is helpful to return to the myth from which the word *narcissism* is derived. Here are translated excerpts of Ovid's version of that myth about the handsome young boy, Narcissus:

Narcissus, weary with hunting, lay down beside a pure untouched spring of silvery water. While he sought to quench his thirst, another thirst grew in him, and as he drank, he was enchanted by the beautiful reflection that he saw. He fell in love with an insubstantial hope, mistaking a mere shadow for a real body. Spellbound by his own reflection, he remained there motionless, with fixed gaze, like a statue carved from Parian marble. As he lay on the bank, he gazed at the twin stars that were his eyes, at his flowing locks, worthy of Bacchus or Apollo, his smooth cheeks, his ivory neck, his lovely face where a rosy flush stained the whiteness of his complexion, admiring all the features for which he himself was admired. Unwittingly, he desired himself, and was himself the object of his own approval, at once seeking and sought, his reflection kindling the flame with which he burned.

How often did he vainly kiss the treacherous pool, how often did he plunge his arms deep into the waters, as he tried to clasp them around the neck he saw there! But he could not hold himself. He did not realize what he was looking at, but was inflamed by the sight, and excited by the very illusion that deceived his eyes.

Staring into the pool, Narcissus wasted away with love. His fair complexion with its rosy flush faded away, gone was his youthful strength, and all the beauties which lately charmed his eyes. Nothing remained of that body which once was. In that same spot, he died. Instead of his corpse, they discovered a flower with a circle of white petals round a yellow center.[1]

Young Narcissus was entranced by the beauty of his reflection upon the water. Nothing else mattered but his image. He was terminally drunk with his impression upon the world and eventually sacrificed himself to that indulgence.

The real tragedy of the myth lies not just in the demise of Narcissus but in his ultimate loss of self. He mistook his reflection for the reality of life. Instead of knowing himself, he experienced his life as it was reflected back to him by his environment. His sense of self was based solely on the water's opinion.

Modern Narcissus

The modern-day Narcissus is transfixed by his reflection from those who surround him. Appearance is extremely important; it is the defining measurement of his soul. In his economy, personal worth is measured by the value assigned to him by others.

He is eager to please as long as pleasing others makes him look good. In fact, he will do almost anything that will maintain the image of success with which he has hopelessly fallen in love. When on the trail of an accolade, all other pursuits are abandoned. Everything in his environment—his job, the company, friends and family—become tools for his glory. When these no longer support his beloved image, they are quickly discarded.

Despite his determination and acquired charisma, the modern Narcissus is not the self-confident person he portrays himself to be. His lack of self-assurance runs deep. He is constantly nagged by feelings of unworthiness and insecurity, feelings that create his insatiable appetite for approval from others.

Here's an updated tale of Narcissus in today's corporation:

Narcissus Goes to Work

Jack's first day on the job was miserable. He had arrived that morning vibrating with enthusiasm, but by lunch he was ready to all but pack up and quit. He quickly surmised that his was the dullest department in the company: data processing.

Printouts of computer code and stacks of manuals in three-ring binders cluttered the office, and in the background was the incessant drone of high-speed printers tapping out the dreary reports that stacked in every corner and on every desk. And to Jack, his coworkers all appeared to be losers. It seemed that most of them would be perfectly happy "treading water" in the data processing department until they retired.

Not Jack. Jack had no intention of staying at the bottom of the corporate ladder one minute longer than he had to. He hadn't scraped through the Ivy League MBA program to be somebody's Bob Cratchet. No, Jack had bigger dreams. As he contemplated his lunch and smiled blankly at the fellow wire-head to whom he was assigned for this get-acquainted lunch, he decided that job one was to get out of the data processing department. Something sexier, like acquisitions or corporate strategy, would suit him much better, he decided. There he could really make a name for himself.

After six months, Jack realized that leaving the "digital dungeon," as he liked to call it, was going to be more difficult than he had expected. As the new guy, he was assigned all the low-visibility grunt work that nobody else wanted. It seemed the only other people with whom he worked outside of his department were equally low on the totem pole and certainly in no position to elevate his stock at the company.

Shortly before his first anniversary with the company, Jack was made a supervisor of the distributed data systems (DDS) project. Along with a slightly bigger cubicle and decent raise, he was given six of his former coworkers to manage, none of whom were particularly happy about their new boss. Jack had campaigned heavily for his new job and, in the process, alienated himself from many of his colleagues. He had become quick to claim credit for ideas that weren't exactly his and equally eager to eliminate the competition by attacking the work of others—some of whom now reported to him.

The DDS project was to be Jack's ticket to stardom.

A complete redesign of the company's primary accounting system, this project would catapult him into practically every office throughout the company, from the president on down. All the major players had a stake in this system, and Jack would be the hero who would make it work for all of them.

He started by arranging a grueling schedule of focus groups. Day after day he met with whole departments, probing into their needs for the system and, much to their amazement, promising incredible results. After each meeting, Jack left voluminous meeting notes on the desks of his staff. It was their job—an increasingly complex task—to sort through these comments and decide how to build a system that accomplished all that Jack had promised. With each meeting the promise list grew to a monumental if not impossible level.

When members of his staff confronted him with the dilemma of writing software to meet so many divergent and sometimes conflicting objectives, he grew visibly agitated. Anything can be done, he would say, if you put your mind to it. (Blaming the messenger was always Jack's response to bad news.) If the code couldn't be written, he seemed to imply, there must be something wrong with the programmer.

Predictably, the staff soon learned to hide the bad news and instead say what Jack wanted to hear. "Great idea Jack! I'll get right on it." This was the only acceptable way to respond.

On top of all the promises Jack had made, he had demanded that the system interface have all the bells and whistles. Fancy screens with lots of buttons and colorful graphs were very important to him. He wanted a look that would sell the system.

Within a year-and-a-half, Jack's staff was ready to roll out the first phase of the system. In reality, it really wasn't a "system" at all. It was a new whiz-bang interface that had been placed on top of the old system. They had given their attention to the look of the interface, ignoring the guts of the system. Sure, with the new system a user could access data with greater ease, but it was the same data, served up by the same slow programs. Jack had merely given the same tired book a brand-new cover.

But it looked great and that was all that counted. Jack relished the "oh's" and "ah's" that inevitably oozed from a group whenever the new system was demonstrated. It would be some time before the users would discover that the new system really didn't do anything that was new, and Jack wasn't concerned. How many of the technology illiterate users in the company would actually figure out that it was the same system? Probably none of them. The system looked new and was, to a small degree, easier to use. That was enough. Enough to get the attention of senior management. Enough to get him a promotion.

Within six months of the complete system roll-out, Jack was whisked up the career ladder to become director of manufacturing operations. This highly visible position put Jack squarely in the center of the corporate spotlight. From there, he could really go places.

Jack had a host of admirable qualities: He was hardworking, energetic, ambitious, and tenacious. No doubt these qualities earned him his promotion.

But Jack also had one fatal flaw: He desperately needed to appear successful. He was more committed to his personal quest for reward and validation than to the well-being of the company or his staff. Maintaining an image of success was paramount in everything he did.

VALIDATE ME—NOW!

This overwhelming need for personal validation is the corporate narcissist's Achilles' heel. Otherwise a stellar employee, the corporate narcissist can always be bribed with the trinkets of personal success. He is insatiable in his need to be admired, and it is this craving that turns a corporation's asset into its worst nightmare.

Jack so wanted the department heads within the company to like him that he was unwilling to place reasonable limits on their requests of the new system. Instead, he agreed to their requests and won their approval, despite the fact that he knew he could never really deliver all that he had promised. At that moment, all that mattered was winning their accolades. Besides, he knew the time between the promise and the system delivery was over two years, and most people would never remember his generous agreements.

Building a functional system that was narrower in scope would have required that Jack take some heat for not fulfilling everyone's wish list. Inevitably, not everyone would be happy with his limits. Although such a system would have been more realistic and, no doubt, far more useful to the company, Jack could not take the personal risk involved. Instead, he opted for a razzle-dazzle makeover of a chronically insufficient system.

Today's successful organization depends upon the willingness of managers to make unpopular decisions and to forgo personal gain in the interest of protecting the long-term future of the company. The corporate narcissist, like Jack, is incapable of such action. His deep-seated need for approval and power prevents him from delaying personal gratification for the greater good.

This is the crux of the problem of corporate narcissism. The personal dilemma of the narcissist bleeds across the lines of personal dysfunction into the realm of work. Every business decision is influenced by the narcissist's extreme needs and cravings. Consequently, what was once the sole concern of a psychotherapist must now be scrutinized in the corporate boardroom. Issues that were once limited to the psychologist's couch have proved to be of great relevance in the everyday working world.

Up Close and Personal

To fully understand narcissism, we must know the history of the narcissist. Most often he has the makings of the ideal corporate citizen: the right schools, the best work experience, notable connections, and perfect recommendations. (After all, the corporate narcissist has been grooming his image for a long time.)

The roots of narcissism go back to some of the earliest experiences of childhood. The adult narcissist develops from the child who learns three basic life lessons:

1. He must be something more than what he is.
2. His value as a person is dependent upon the image he projects.
3. Other people are objects who must be manipulated to get the validation he needs.

As a child, the adult narcissist never experienced unconditional acceptance. He was rewarded and embraced only when fulfilling the expectations of his caregivers. When the child, and later the young adult, was himself, he was never smart enough, confident enough, or skillful enough. Affection was linked to his being the child his parents needed him to be.

This lack of what psychologist Carl Rogers called unconditional positive regard has a profound effect on the life of the narcissist. At a critical point in her psychological development she was deprived of the necessary validation of self. Without this validation, a strong sense of self never developed. The narcissist finds herself caught in an endless search for the persons who will give her the unconditional acceptance she never experienced.

The narcissist roams the psychological landscape searching for something she will never find. She may indeed find unconditional acceptance, but it never repairs the hole created by her early life deprivations. Her craving for acceptance, validation, and praise is insatiable; no matter how much she receives, it is never enough.

Like rain and sun to a seed, the self must have unconditional acceptance to germinate and grow into a strong sense of personal identity. Without that acceptance during the critical time of childhood, the seed turns dormant and fails to sprout. For the narcissist the self ceases to develop.

Since the narcissist carries no internal definition of who he is, what he feels, and how he should be, he scans the expectations of those in authority and composes a self that would most surely be worthy of acceptance, and this he tries to become. He arranges his life and all its accouterments into a personal masterpiece. He earns a degree in the field of study with the most potential for success. He drives the car that makes the right statement about his attitude and status. He frequents the social clubs where he can make the best contacts. Everything about his life is engineered to reflect the image of what he wishes to be.

For all of his ambition, the narcissist fails to develop the unique aspects of his real self. He knows no passion other than achieving success in others' eyes. He lacks a strong sense of personal values and direction and incapable of deep emotion. Worst of all, his own self-alienation prevents him from empathizing with the feelings of others.

MAGIC MIRRORS

The narcissist is simply addicted to the image he has created. More to the point, he is transfixed by the *reflection* of that image. He arranges his life around mirrors—other people who reflect the image of himself he wishes to see. At work, the narcissist demands complete loyalty from his mirrors. He demands that they agree with his decisions and support his actions. In whatever they do or say, they are required to make him look good.

Not surprisingly, the narcissist cannot tolerate criticism from others. Criticism in its mildest form is experienced as a direct personal attack. Every social interaction is a referendum on his acceptability and anything less than an affirmative response is a negative vote. He sees people as either with him or against him; there is no middle ground.

The narcissist can be highly threatened by others who do not collude in his game of image. Even the smallest differences of opinion can elicit a storm of his anger. His ego, while seemingly overblown, is very fragile. To protect himself, he must strike back at the opposition and eliminate it. The narcissist often has a long memory of those he feels have offended him.

MANIPULATE OR BE MANIPULATED

For the narcissist, manipulating others is a way of life. Others exist, for the most part, to fulfill his wishes. Friends and associates are of value as long as they help him get what he wants. Once they are no longer useful, he drops them.

This seemingly cold and calculated way of dealing with others is rooted in the narcissist's own undeveloped self. Since he knows little of his own feelings, he cannot empathize with the feelings of others. To the narcissist, feelings are foreign, even frivolous.

The truth is, he has never been able to empathize with the feelings of others. Because he long ago learned to bury his true self underneath a veneer of a more acceptable self, he never developed a familiarity with the depth of his own feelings; consequently, he is unable to feel the emotions of others in any meaningful way. He can understand the *idea* of others' emotions, but he doesn't know what they must *feel* like, for he has rarely felt them within himself. Like a slow strangle of the soul, he has lost the capacity to feel all but the most primitive emotions of joy and grief that, because of their overwhelming force, cannot be denied. His own emotional bankruptcy prevents him from identifying with the feelings of others and allows him to be at home with manipulation.

Without a doubt, the narcissist's lack of empathy creates his monstrous side, especially when he attains a position of authority. Here he can execute his plans with machine-like efficiency. If it makes him look like the best CEO, he can lay off thousands of employees, close down plants and destroy communities with little notice, ship jobs to countries where adults are paid pennies a day and children are a substantial portion of the labor force, blatantly harm the environment, or knowingly destroy the health of consumers. Because he cannot feel the pain he causes as he strives for success, he is blind to the negative results of that quest.

THE VICIOUS CYCLE

The narcissist is caught in the grip of a vicious cycle. He desperately needs approval and acceptance, but because he is unwilling to risk possible rejection, he must force others, his mirrors, into subservient admiration. In time, the mirrors come to resent his domination and abandon him, fulfilling his deepest fears of rejection. He must then find new and more loyal mirrors—and the cycle continues.

The narcissist is incapable of breaking out of this cycle. He cannot see that if he were to allow his real self to show in all of its flawed glory, others would be drawn to his sincerity and genuineness. He fails to see how his ruthless manipulation of others only pushes them farther away and creates ill-will instead of the acceptance he needs. Rather than allowing true admiration to grow, he tries to steal it, and in the process kills whatever genuine regard may have existed.

THE NARCISSIST'S PAIN

Life for the corporate narcissist is painful. He is riddled with feelings of emptiness and insatiable needs that drive him relentlessly. On the surface, he may appear to have it all; but a simple scratch beneath the surface tells a very different story. Consider the true story of Roger:

Roger's office was always the picture of perfection and organization. No papers on the desk, no sticky notes above the credenza, no family pictures or children's drawings taped to the wall. On the clean desk were a computer screen, computer mouse, and desktop calendar. Two nicely framed pictures hung on the walls, each in symmetrical alignment with the corners of the room. At one end of the office was a conference table with a spotless surface. All of Roger's work was filed away under a regimented filing system so that any document could be accessed immediately. Anyone who saw the office couldn't help but feel that whoever occupied it was on top and in control.

Roger's appearance was no less neat and professional. He had a magnificent wardrobe from the most expensive men's clothing stores, and always wore a starched white shirt, conservative tie, designer wool pants, and Italian leather lace-up shoes. Although the company had a policy of casual dress, Roger preferred to dress in a manner he considered more professional. Accessorized with an antique tank watch and designer wire-rimmed glasses, he presented an image that projected his taste for success.

Roger was a manager of human resources for a group of over 5,000 employees. He worked his way up to this powerful post from a clerical position, earning his undergraduate degree along the way. He had a staff of more than twenty employees in his department, which controlled all of the human resources issues for the site. There were only two human resources jobs that were more powerful.

Roger had a remarkable mastery of "corporate speak." The right words for any situation just spilled from his mouth. As in most human resources jobs, heated arguments and sticky situations were common, and Roger handled each situation without losing his cool or missing a beat. He seemed to know exactly what to say to get his point across and convince his listener. He held his own whether it was with a vice-president or a janitor.

Roger was a narcissist. The office, the clothes, and the manner of speech were just a few of the tools he used to portray an image of success and achievement. Senior managers could always count on Roger to get the job done.

The first time I remember seeing this in action was when Roger was a human resources manager for a considerably smaller division. Roger had formed a close working relationship with the general manager of the division, who had a reputation as a mover and a shaker. The division was under considerable pressure to bring to market in the next six months a product that had been in development for several years. To do this, the general manager needed a much larger staff of software engineers. Consequently, he and Roger worked out a plan to dramatically increase hiring into the division. During the same period, however, all of the human resources managers in the company were asked to bring all new hiring to a halt because the company was not performing as expected. Using a loophole in the company's policy regarding new hires, Roger was able to hire twenty-five new engineers. Needless to say, the general manager was elated that Roger had been so responsive to his needs, and as a result, Roger was given a promotion and a salary increase.

Within a year, virtually every one of the new engineers had to be relocated or laid off. Just as he had been warned might happen, the company had to take drastic measures to reduce costs and began a layoff program based on tenure. Roger could have followed the guidelines and not hired the engineers, but that would have had no glory. Instead, he chose to ally himself with a general manager's own need to be successful and to hire the extra staff. Roger's short-term success with the general manager eventually cost the company an enormous amount and played havoc in those new employees' lives. Interestingly enough, the general manager blamed the layoffs not on Roger but on the company's "antiquated" human resources policies.

Roger often joked with me about his eligibility for a Taurus automobile, the company car. When employees reached a certain salary grade (one level above Roger's current level), they were given a Taurus to drive. Because very few managers were given company cars, those who did were known to have powerful positions. Despite the fact that he had a new car that he loved, getting a company car was very important to Roger. He tried everything he could to get a Taurus. He even took on extra responsibilities and hired additional subordinates so that he could make the argument that his salary grade needed to be raised a level (despite the fact that such a move would not affect his already above-range salary).

More than once he brought this situation to the attention of his superiors. Driving a company-owned Taurus was a symbol of power Roger needed, not for material benefit but for ego enhancement.

As an internal management consultant, I worked closely with Roger for several years when he confided two secrets to me. First, he admitted that he often hated his job. On a good day, he was ambivalent; the rest of the time, he dreaded work. Roger approached his job with such energy and attention that no one would ever guess he disliked the job. He was always on top of every issue, constantly pushing his staff to do the same. Roger was in the office early, rarely took lunch breaks, and left late almost every day. He was the exemplary manager.

Roger had always wanted to be a chef. A weekend gourmet and connoisseur of fine foods, he had a genuine love for cooking. I remember Roger telling me he once made four consecutive batches of beef Wellington and threw each one away until he finally got it exactly right on the fourth try. He truly enjoyed the culinary arts.

Roger had denied his passion for cooking for a career in business shortly after entering college. For all but the highly successful, the gastronomic profession pays rather meagerly, so he chose a career with more lucrative promise.

Interestingly enough, about a year after he told me of his avocation, Roger had the opportunity to follow his dream. The company, trying yet again to reduce costs, offered a severance package to anyone who wanted to leave. The package was based on the number of years an employee had with the company and could add up to a significant amount for someone who had been there as long as Roger. He calculated that it would give him enough money to pay off his debts and make it through the culinary academy. He seriously entertained the idea and went so far as to tell his boss's boss about his idea. While this may sound like a risky move, Roger had already calculated the odds and decided he would win no matter what the outcome. If she accepted his leaving, he would take the package and resign.

On the other hand, she might just "up the ante" and offer him a promotion.

Much to the pleasure of Roger's needy ego, his boss's superior first tested his resolve by trying to convince him to stay. When she realized that wasn't working, she asked what it would take for him to remain. Pleased that she had fulfilled his fantasies about this situation, he insisted that he be given his boss's job. Within two months, she fired his boss, and the job was his. He now had a more powerful position, the coveted Taurus, more pay, and a job he liked even less.

Roger was bright and motivated. When he wanted something, he could even be charming. He had been successful at every job he had been given, and by all standards, had a very successful career. Yet Roger would complain to me privately about feeling empty and tired. At times he would talk of walking away from it all and doing something he really wanted to do. He felt trapped by the knowledge that he would be unable to make his current salary doing anything else and by the memory of all the hard work he had invested in attaining his position. He gleaned some satisfaction from the periodic pay raises and promotions, but for the most part, work devoid of meaning for him. Because he spent so much time and energy at work, dissatisfaction at work meant dissatisfaction with life.

Roger's story is not unlike the story of many corporate narcissists. While his designs could be devastating to those around him, he was never intentionally mean-spirited. His strategies were simply one-sided in their attempt to propel his career forward. His own emotional drought prevented him from seeing the hurt he inflicted on those he rolled over.

Roger had created a vicious cycle for himself. The more powerful the position he attained, the more necessary it was to convince himself that it was right for him. The more he denied his true feelings and desires, the more he needed the trappings of success to overcome a sense of worthlessness and powerlessness over his own life. The elevated salary became the golden handcuffs that chained him to a life that wasn't what he really wanted but was necessary to feed his narcissistic needs.

Just as Roger passed up the opportunity to leave his job and go to the culinary academy, narcissists are rarely able to break the cycle that enslaves them. I'm sure Roger must have had nightmares when he imagined the possibility that he would graduate from the academy and go to work in the back room of a restaurant as the underling of a more experienced chef, or perhaps that he might fail as a chef and be doomed to the life of a short-order cook. Such a situation would strip away the mask and bring him face-to-face with a vulnerable part of himself. This threat is what keeps the narcissist on the treadmill of his never-ending endeavor to be something he isn't.

To this day Roger works as a human resources executive for the same company. He is still very successful; perhaps he has resigned himself to a life of working in a position that feeds his narcissistic needs.

PERSONAL FACADE

Like Roger, many narcissists report feeling empty or hollow. Despite their efforts to convince others of their value and significance, they never really succeed at convincing themselves. This ever-haunting knowledge that they are a counterfeit, that they are not who they have created, leaves them with many unanswered questions: Who am I? What do I want out of life? Why am I spending all of my time doing something that doesn't really matter?

The answers to these questions would seem to lead the narcissists out of their self defeating cycle; in reality, they often only lead to more narcissistic behavior. If they will only work harder and be more successful, then they will feel as if they have accomplished something of great significance and merit. They fool themselves into thinking they must play the game even harder to attain any satisfaction and contentment. Narcissists may also blame those around them for their feelings of inadequacy. If only they weren't surrounded by people who drag them down and hinder their accomplishments! The narcissist thinks, if people would only do things my way, then I could be truly successful and accomplish great things.

Narcissists frequently put off for tomorrow the haunting personal questions that can not be answered today. Once I make vice-president, or make a fortune, or retire, then I will have time to spend with the grandchildren, or to work for charity, or to learn to paint. The narcissist will swear that he is only doing what he must so that he will be able, some time in the future, to do those things that are meaningful. One narcissist told me that when he retired he was going to buy a farm and just watch the grass grow. When he did retire, he spent six long months of watching the grass grow; then he ran for the county board of supervisors. His need for validation overwhelmed the retirement he had planned for decades.

The narcissist creates a working environment that lacks trust, then finds that others often mistrust her in return. The narcissist finds herself locked out of the informal, social circle at the office. Others may treat her with kindness and social grace, but they aren't inclined to include her in the casual gossip session or the after-work hangout. They aren't about to confide in someone who may use what she hears against them at some time in the future. Because she had no experience with such trusting relationships in the past, the narcissist doesn't understand why she is left out.

Almost all narcissists harbor deep feelings of isolation and alienation, much like the teacher's pet who has been left on the playground to play by himself. He so wants to win the friendship of his classmates, but his overwhelming need for praise and recognition from the teacher always gets in the way. Eventually, he may decide that he doesn't need friendship and that others reject him out of jealously for his superior abilities. Similarly, the narcissist will most likely decide that all such social behavior is only for those whose careers aren't going anywhere anyway. After all, he wasn't hired to make friends.

The narcissist's plight is a tragic one. It is painful to the narcissist and equally caustic for those who must operate within his world. Once the narcissist enters the organization and attains a position of power, he can spread his poison throughout every aspect of the business. Chapter Two looks at the narcissist as corporate manager and the profound effect he can have within his sphere of organizational influence.

TWO

Building the Empire: Management Style of a Narcissist

One of the hardest lessons to learn for a business person trained in the mental health field as I was is that a psychologically healthy employee is not necessarily a more productive employee. Sometimes, just the opposite is true. For example, a slightly obsessive-compulsive accountant or quality engineer can be quite good for the company. A security manager with a touch of paranoia or a workaholic sales rep can be true assets. On the other hand, persons with healthier psyches may no longer be willing to work on the weekend or travel on business and be away from their children for weeks at a time. Good mental health does not always equal a good employee.

It is with this very important fact in mind that we explore the world of the narcissistic manager. We must reach beyond the personal tragedies of the narcissist and find out just what effect this psychological state has on the performance of the organization. If narcissism is an important issue for business, it must be shown to have an effect on the performance of the enterprise.

Without a doubt, it does. An out-of-control narcissist promoted to a position of power can kill the most prosperous of companies. Most often this silent killer slips unnoticed through the back door and does irreparable damage before he can be stopped. The narcissistic management style is insidiously toxic.

THE COST OF NARCISSISM

The first time I remember coming face-to-face with the work of a narcissist, I was staring at the cool, gray gun-metal of a revolver held in a trembling hand.

"I donna want to do it, I donna want to do it," he told me in broken English.

"I dream it, but I donna want to do it."

The small Portuguese immigrant was huddled in the corner. He hung his head and tears flowed and he rocked slightly back and forth. Not much was in the supply room where he had taken himself hostage: a few chairs, a dust-mop, and a few patches of light coming from a forgotten window.

Only moments earlier I had been telephoned by Salo, manager of the maintenance department, to take care of an unfortunate circumstance. "Would you mind coming immediately?" Salo had said with an overly controlled voice. Throughout my years in human resources, I had heard this tone from other managers in trouble, and I knew it well. I headed straight for Salo's office.

When I entered the department area, Salo led me to a supply closet, opened the door, and walked away. That's when I saw Roberto with the gun.

Roberto kept saying over and over, "I donna want to do it."

"What?" I said as gently as I could muster. "What don't you want to do?"

Roberto sat rocking back and forth, at first oblivious to my presence. Only after what seemed to be ten minutes did he acknowledge me with his eyes. Over the next hour we progressed from my nervous chatter and his faint mumbling to something of a conversation. Roberto's English was excellent for someone who had lived in the States for only four years, but on the whole it was broken and insufficient to communicate what he had to say. This was why, I realized, he had resorted to the universal language of flashing a gun: He wanted to be heard.

I asked Roberto for the gun and without hesitation (and much to my relief), he handed it to me. There was something in his gentle manner that told me he had never intended to use the gun. He only used it for punctuation—to provoke the attention he had been otherwise unable to rouse. With the danger aside, we sat and talked. I wanted to know what had brought all of this about.

Roberto told me that he had worked for the last four years in the maintenance department. They had been tough years, but as he reminded me again and again, he was no stranger to hard work. It wasn't the hard work but the constant belittling and endless pushing from Salo that had become unbearable. Salo would demand that a job be done over many times until it met his perfectionist standards. No, it wasn't the hard work. This was about honor and respect. Salo had given no respect and treated his subordinates as a subhuman species. For a hardworking Portuguese immigrant like Roberto, honor was all he had. This was what brought him to the brink.

To everyone except his employees, Salo was a shining example of what determination and hard work can accomplish. Salo had been born and raised on a small and very poor Portuguese island in the Atlantic. He had moved with his wife and children to the United States to look for a better life. The family arrived with no formal education and no marketable skills and spoke no English. They lived with cousins while he and his wife hurriedly tried to find some means of support. Salo eventually taught himself English and found a position as a janitor with a large high tech company. Over a series of ten years, Salo went back to school at night, first earning a high school diploma equivalency and then going on to finish a four-year college degree in business administration. During those ten years, Salo worked equally hard at his day job. He was promoted to janitorial supervisor, and by the time he had earned his degree, he was manager of the entire facility's department for a site of 3,500 employees.

No question about it, the company could count on Salo. It was well known in the company that Salo's site was the best maintained site in the company (even if it was the oldest). He prided himself on the fact that he could see his reflection in the highly polished floors anywhere in the series of six buildings on the site. He ran a tight ship. Every request was responded to promptly and appropriately.

I remember a very dramatic example of his incredible persistence and drive. Five-hundred people on the site were to be moved from one building to another. The group, a twenty-four-hour customer service operation, had to be moved without any disruption in service, which meant that the move had to be perfectly planned and executed in a very small period of time. Anyone who has been through the ordeal of an office move knows that is virtually impossible, but Salo had the move complete and picture-perfect in less than twelve hours over one night. When the site managers arrived the next morning, no one could believe it. Every phone, every file cabinet, every manual was right where it was supposed to be. You could always count on Salo.

In spite of all his laurels, Salo was a narcissistic manager, and the company was paying an enormous cost for his image of success. Not only did it push an otherwise dedicated employee to the extreme; it cost the company several million dollars.

Since most of Salo's employees spoke limited English and had few marketable skills, they were thankful to have jobs. Salo, however, used this to his advantage. He demanded that his employees work many hours of overtime without pay or risk losing their jobs. Not knowing anything different and unwilling to jeopardize their employment, his employees complied.

Eventually, however, the strain became too great, and one employee filed suit for back pay. Before long, almost a hundred current and former employees joined the litigation, and the company was forced to negotiate a costly settlement.

THE CHARACTERISTICS OF NARCISSISM

Narcissistic managers are to be found in virtually every company in America. The footprints they leave behind make them easy to identify and track. Their narcissistic behavior is so commonplace and businesslike, one might not see them for looking past them. A few of their characteristics follow.

Workaholic

Narcissistic managers usually work extremely long hours. They are classic workaholics, sacrificing all other aspects of their personal lives to spend all their time and energy at work. Time away from work is usually spent strategizing and thinking about work. It is not uncommon for a narcissistic manager to schedule meetings in the early morning or evening hours, expecting that others keep the same pace. They plan vacations around work activities, if they take them at all. Only in cases of exceptional illness will narcissists take time off—and then they work from home.

Loyal to the Company

Narcissistic managers profess loyalty to the company and its values. They work hard to be informed with the latest information about the business and its performance. It isn't uncommon for narcissistic managers to maintain professional contacts outside the company to stay up-to-date on the latest in their field. Neither is holding office nor speaking to professional organizations unusual for narcissistic managers. They are eager to take on increased responsibilities and work hard to establish a reputation deserving of increased accountability. The zenith of character in a narcissistic manager's eyes is to

be seen as someone who gets the job done. He will work end-
lessly to be viewed as such.

All of these qualities are highly valued, sought-after traits
in managers. American business schools have adopted these
attributes as the foundation for training management students. The political and reward systems of most organizations
are geared to identify and promote such individuals. Most
managerial performance appraisal systems measure these
qualities explicitly and tie pay increases and bonus money to
the ratings. There is hardly a business manager around who
would disagree that the person thus described has excellent
potential for success as a manager.

When the volume on these fine characteristics is turned
up past a reasonable level—as it is in narcissism—what was
once an attribute becomes an organizational stumbling block.
The following are the negative traits of narcissism that develop
as the narcissist indulges her needs for recognition and power.

Uses Resources to His Own Advantage

More concerned for his career than the long-term interest of the company, the toll the narcissistic manager exacts is
heavy. While he gets things done, he stops at nothing to get
the job accomplished. So committed is he to his success and
reputation, he spends whatever time, money, and talent it
takes to make the job appear a success once he has begun.
He is not one to admit failure, even when that failure was
unforeseen or due to unexpected circumstances. He can be
excessively controlling and often uses up very creative and talented staff members in a short time. The narcissist is inflexible and intolerant of differing viewpoints, and views his staff
as an extension of his arm in carrying out his agenda. He is
slow to change his opinions and actively thwarts any move that
might reduce his power. In short, he is a one-man company
who is in business to promote himself. He uses whatever resources and power the company gives him to his advantage.

Need for Power

A high need for power over other people is quite evident
in the style of the narcissistic manager. He uses accepted

management techniques to increase his span of control over the people and events that surround him. He is driven to build an ever increasing power base that will help mitigate his personal sense of powerlessness over the self. To fulfill his ever gnawing need for power, the narcissistic manager uses three key techniques: manipulating others, controlling communications and information, and controlling decision making.

Manipulation of Others

The first technique, manipulation of others, is the most commonly used and, ironically, most resented technique of the narcissistic management style. The narcissistic manager denies the humanity of others, choosing to view them as objects, or modules, to be moved about the game board of the organization. Those who enter the playing field become pawns to be manipulated at will. While the narcissistic manager is virtually incapable of an empathic response to the needs and feelings of other people, he clearly understands the value of manipulating them.

For example, when he asks for an employee's opinion, he does it not to understand or learn from the employee, but to discover how to convince the employee of his idea. Narcissists desperately need other people to carry out their schemes and to mirror back the excellency of their talents and, as such, realize the value of motivating others to support their plans. They may turn on considerable charm, sympathy, or understanding if necessary to ensnare another. When the pawn has served his purposes and is of no further use, he is coolly discarded.

By the time a narcissist has become a manager, he has learned the art of manipulation in its highest form. Truly an artist, the accomplished narcissist will pull unsuspecting employees into his ploy and use them for his purposes with such subtlety and finesse that they may be unaware of the manipulation. He weaves complex schemes to make others think that they are fulfilling his expectations of their own will. It is the art of "reverse psychology": creating a situation that causes another to think and act in ways that you desire.

The narcissistic manager often assumes that others are just as comfortable with manipulation and that they, too, use others for personal advancement. He often sees others as wanting something from him and is highly sensitized to being used by someone else. Interactions with others in the company usually take the form of a tradeoff: "If I give you what you need, what do I get in return?" Conversely, when he needs something from others, he assumes that others will require some tradeoff from him. It is not unusual for the narcissistic manager to stockpile power and resources to use as bargaining chips when needed.

Taking action solely for the good of the company or another person is simply not enough. Unless there is something to be gained in the way of increased visibility or positive image, the narcissistic manager is unlikely to do it. On the rare occasion that he does act without reciprocation, an IOU is created that is sure to be cashed.

MANIPULATIVE PLOT TWIST

One of the most blatant examples of narcissistic manipulation I can remember witnessing occurred when I was working as a consultant to a large utility company in the western United States. My motivation for taking the company as a client was to work for Donna, who had a reputation as one of the finest industrial psychologists in the area. Donna grew up on the streets of New York City and later became a high school English teacher. She was very articulate, assertive, street-smart, and compassionate. She had quickly gained an excellent professional reputation within the company, which included frequent consultations with the CEO. Within two years of her hiring, Donna's boss, an extreme narcissist, had become threatened by her independence of thought. She was unwilling to pay homage to his pet programs simply because he had approved them. With consummate professionalism, she would attempt to challenge his thinking and reason a better solution, which, of course, would send him into a narcissistic rage. Excepting Donna, he had surrounded himself with a staff of well-meaning, well-educated professionals who carried out his ideas exactly as he dictated. He had little interest in learning from anyone, much less Donna.

One day I got a call from Donna. As soon as I stepped into her office, I could tell from her smile that she had good news. She shut the door behind us and began describing for me a new position that had been created for her. The position would be a promotion and would allow her to focus almost exclusively on executive development, her favorite area of work. For impending business reasons, she would occupy the new position and her replacement would begin immediately.

After all the company announcements had been made and Donna's replacement had begun the staff transition, Ron, her boss, made his move. He called Donna to his office, briefly apologized, then coolly relayed that he had not gotten proper approval for her new position and that his tardy request for that approval had been denied. Simply put, she was out of a job. Within a week a severance package was negotiated and Donna was laid off. Ron had effectively eliminated a roadblock to his eminence while the company *paid* to lose one its finest talents.

The manipulative nature of Ron's actions toward Donna showed a lack of understanding and empathy for what it must feel like to have expectations raised and then subsequently dashed. Nevertheless, he did it because firing Donna outright would have most likely led to a costly lawsuit that the company could not have won given the unfounded nature of the termination. Consequently, Ron devised a plan that would eliminate the negative visibility of a lawsuit and remove a thorn from his side.

Undoubtedly, Ron considered the impact of such manipulation on Donna and her staff and the resulting anger and frustration only as far as it could affect him. What harm could that anger bring to his carefully crafted reputation? His decisions and actions following Donna's firing were calculated on these odds. Anyone who would have considered how it must feel to be brutally tricked out of a livelihood could not have taken the course of action Ron took. Similarly, the narcissistic manager has little capacity to identify with the emotions of others.

Manipulation Breeds Resentment

While the narcissistic manager may gain the respectful attention of those he works with, he also builds resentment and distrust among those he manipulates. With a healthy respect for what he can accomplish and an awareness of what can happen if he is crossed, others will be cordial and generally compliant with his requests. Because he is a stranger to trusting relationships, the narcissistic manager hasn't a clue that anything is missing from his work relationships.

A quality manager of a midwestern manufacturing firm was charged with the task of introducing a major company-wide quality initiative. He assigned the project of selecting a vendor of total quality training to one of his quality engineers, then found himself in the situation of disagreeing with the vendor choice the engineer had made. He made several attempts to make the engineer come around to his way of thinking, but was unable to convince her. Together they reviewed her plan point by point, but was unable to produce convincing evidence that his plan was better, since both plans were equally strong on the conceptual and statistical elements. After some time of impasse, he decided to temporarily forgo his opinions and allowed her to pursue the plan she had devised. In a rare show of graciousness, he allowed her total control of the project, going out of his way to show her independence and empowerment.

She independently prepared the necessary presentation

for the company's executive committee. After reviewing her presentation materials, he chose to not comment on what he knew was a fatal flaw. She had prepared the presentation around the conceptual elements of the program, something the executive committee had not responded to positively in the past. Several days later, she made the presentation and just as he expected, the committee rejected her recommendations. At that point, he interrupted and took the floor to present the statistical elements of the program he originally supported, winning their approval. Afterwards he dismissed her disappointment by insisting that the meeting went well. After all, he said, they did get approval to set up a quality program!

Without obvious coercion or strong-arming, he had accomplished three things. First and most obvious, he had succeeded in getting his ideas implemented. Unable to convince his own staff member of his ideas, he had used a higher-powered group, the executive committee, to do so. At the end, it was not he who had chosen to carry out his plan, but the executive committee. Furthermore, he appeared as the knight in shining armor, saving the day. It was a highly visible move in front of the most powerful group in the company that undoubtedly testified to his superior abilities. Finally, he taught this engineer a lesson without ever saying a word. Follow his path, implement his ideas, and you will be protected and successful. You can be assured it was a long time before that engineer opposed him again.

No one knows for sure what would have happened had he supported her recommendation by helping her modify the presentation in the first place. Since he knew the decision would hinge as much on the presentation's approach as the actual content, he could have helped her reframe her ideas into a presentation style that would have been likely to win approval. Such action would have helped her develop her skills and confidence and would have fulfilled the objective of setting up a total quality program. Unfortunately, it would not have met his narcissistic need to see his ideas thrive and for him personally to receive the credit for those ideas in front of the executive committee. He had fulfilled his needs at the cost of promoting an employee's development. To top it all off, he had done it all under the guise of doing what was best for the business.

Imagine how that quality engineer felt after she was humiliated in front of the executive committee or how she must feel about a supervisor who knowingly allowed her to fail for the sake of his own agenda. He had forced her into a career-limiting corner, and the only way out was the path he had chosen for her. Puppeteering charity, the kind of help that destroys one's freedom of choice, always creates mistrust and resentment toward the "helper" and, as in this example, destroys the bond of mutual commitment and service between employee and employer.

CONTROLLING COMMUNICATIONS AND INFORMATION

Another power technique used by the narcissistic manager is the control of communications and information flow. Much like the work of a public relations agent, the narcissistic manager is busy creating a salable image of himself. While part of that process means acting in ways that are consistent with the image, another large part is controlling what is communicated to the organization about him and his department. Actions and events can mean many things, and the narcissistic manager is keenly aware of his ability to affect how others interpret his actions.

Putting a Spin on Setbacks

Warren, a manufacturing manager, headed the largest manufacturing division of a large defense contractor. Not only did he have the largest staff; he controlled most of the company's premier product lines, including several highly touted new products. His boss was nearing retirement and Warren had an eye on a promotion to his job, the highest-ranking manufacturing job in the company. To raise his potential for the job in a company that was heavily dependent on federal regulations, Warren arranged a highly visible, one-year, corporate-sponsored fellowship in the department of defense. Several months after arriving in Washington, something went very wrong (no one seems to know exactly what), and Warren found himself needing his old job back nearly six months earlier than planned. Upon return to the company, however, Warren was given the only manufacturing job open, which was in one of the oldest divisions in the company, a much smaller and far less prestigious position. To try to correct the perception of this failure, Warren publicized the story that he had been called back from Washington early to solve the division's manufacturing problems (of which no one was aware) and to broaden his experience before accepting the vice presidential position.

The narcissistic manager can put a spin on almost any event if it is to his advantage. Like Warren, he takes whatever the outcome and spins a story that fulfills the plot he has invented. Should events turn out less than desirable, he becomes the master of damage control, issuing virtual press releases by the hour until the danger is passed. The story is easily recognizable; it has an airtight goodness about it that makes it super-real. The narcissistic manager must always appear in control and successful, even heroic.

Rewriting the Mail

It is not uncommon for the narcissistic manager to insist on reviewing all written communications issuing from his department. I have known more than one who reserves a red pen for editing staff memos. One extremely frustrated employee of a narcissistic manager showed me a file of documents two inches thick that were covered in red ink. "He bled all over them!" she exclaimed.

Another curious practice narcissistic managers use is that of writing memos or letters for other people. By writing the letter and then forwarding it to the "sender" for their signature, he ensures that his ideas and intent aren't muddled with another's "misunderstanding." Obviously, this tactic is most often used between a narcissistic manager and subordinate.

The narcissistic manager is insistent upon complete and regular updates and needs to be informed about all activities in his department. Staff meetings can look more like interrogations, as every detail of a project is reviewed with a fine-tooth comb. He needs to be completely informed at all times, in the event that he, in turn, is questioned about some remote aspect of a project. To be unable to respond might suggest that he was not in complete control of what was happening in his department and would hinder his accepting credit for any success that might result. On the flip side, employees learn that there is a very practical reason for keeping him completely informed. Rather than appear ignorant, he may invent an explanation on the spot and commit to deliverables and time lines that may not have been planned.

Controlling Meetings

Meetings are the perfect opportunity for the narcissistic manager to control the flow of information in the department. Before meetings, he will prep any of his staff members in on the meeting, telling them his opinion on the topic of discussion. He does so with the expectation that his staff will work with him and show support for his ideas.

During the meeting, there are several tricks he may use to ensure it goes his way. The most common ploy is the narcissistic filibuster: talking at length until any remaining opposition is exhausted, and, as a result, compliant. Another tactic he may use is to talk around the subject in abstract and complex terms to intimidate those present into thinking that they have missed important information or, perhaps, lack the intelligence to follow the conversation. He may also use analogies and metaphors that lend his opinions an air of common sense and truth. Finally, it is not uncommon for him to spend extraordinary time, effort, and money on elaborate and painstakingly prepared presentations to ensure agreement from his audience.

A TALE OF TWO NARCISSISTS

Mike, a research and development manager, and Cecil, a resident business consultant, were the perfect example of a pair of narcissists manipulating a meeting. Mike was in charge of implementing the company-wide program to cut costs that Cecil had been hired to design. Both Mike and Cecil were well-educated and articulate. The cost cutting program involved examining every department in the company through a series of meetings between Mike, Cecil, and the department managers. The meetings started with the department managers presenting the projects for which they were responsible and the rationale for each project. At the end of the presentations, Mike and Cecil took control of the discussion about which projects should stay and which should go.

When the department managers attempted to enter this discussion, Mike and Cecil almost immediately dismissed their comments by referring to documents the managers had not seen or decisions of which the managers had been unaware. If the opposition persisted, Mike and Cecil worked together to discredit the others. The last half of this all-day meeting ultimately ended with Mike and Cecil redesigning the work flow of the department, each trying to be more clever in his ideas than the other. In true narcissistic form, a document published after the meeting showed what decisions the *group* had ostensibly agreed upon.

CONTROL AND DECISION MAKING AT THE LOWEST LEVELS

Narcissistic managers are notorious for controlling all decision making within their department. The narcissistic manager, no matter how high in the organization, will at times involve himself in decisions that are the responsibility of several levels

below. Because he maintains tight control over himself, he
naturally exerts control over many of the details, never trusting the judgments of those beneath him. He is a stranger to
the trust that is a necessary ingredient for empowering employees.

Trusting those who work for you goes a step higher than
merely delegating tasks. Trust means delegating the responsibility and authority to complete a task and allowing another to
make decisions, knowing that this person will do everything
possible to make decisions that are successful. Trust means
giving enough room to allow another to make decisions that
may not be the same decisions you would make. The basis for
trust is knowing that while everyone brings something different and valuable to the table, you are all committed to the
ultimate objective and will work together to achieve it.

Narcissistic Trust

In contrast, the narcissistic manager defines trust differently. For the narcissist, trust is an employee who will espouse
his ideas and make similar decisions to his own. After all, he
alone knows what is best. His valued employees function as
extensions of himself by adhering to his agenda; these are the
only employees worthy of his "trust."

It isn't always easy for him to find someone who is willing
to think and act just like he does. It is an endless source of
frustration to him that some employees are simply unable to
read his mind. The best that he can do is hire one or two
clones of himself and work constantly at keeping the rest on
track.

There are a number of ways the narcissistic manager con-
trols his image through his staff. One of his most effective
techniques at uncovering inconsistencies is to perform random inquiries. Walking through the department asking about
this paper or that file, listening to bits and pieces of phone
conversations, and conducting friendly chats with employees
about the day's activities enable him to perform a random
quality control and make sure that all is aligned with his
wishes. When he encounters misalignment, no matter how

small or trivial the task, he may engage in an immediate and on-the-spot repair by giving directions to correct the error. To him it is irrelevant that the employee is operating according to the direction of another supervisor or is pursuing his own method of accomplishing the objective at hand. The narcissist views the department as a collective mirror that exists to reflect his image, and all others must bow to this rule.

Curve Ball

One of the more subtle methods of controlling subordinates is the "curve ball." When a subordinate seems to be out of his control and acting independently, the manager makes a decision that is perplexingly uncharacteristic. The department grinds to halt as his staff tries to figure out just what is going on. Why did he do *that*? Everyone is thrown off balance by his unpredictability, and this places them solidly back under his control. Suddenly, everyone wants to get a read from him before they move. This is exactly the kind of control he needs.

A clear example of this happened when Joe T., the senior vice president of merchandising for a large retailer, began working closely with the men's clothing buyer who, although part of his division, was three management levels below him. Joe had been publicly challenged by this aggressive buyer on a previous issue, and decided it was time to involve himself in this buyer's business. The buyer had just placed a large order for men's flannel shirts that had been selling quite well over the past several winter seasons. The VP didn't have to look far to find an opportunity to knock this buyer's decision to renew the flannel shirt order. The buttons were all wrong! Although these were the same buttons that had always been specified for these shirts, Joe aggressively questioned the buyer's judgment in using them and changed the order to a slightly more expensive button, despite a company strategy that had been enacted to keep costs down on this type of product. Further, he insisted these buttons be used on all future orders. Perplexed and bewildered, the buyer followed his directive. The vice president threw an unexpected, although effective, curveball just to remind the buyer who really was in control.

EMPIRE BUILDING

Using his well-practiced power techniques, the narcissistic manager will "build an empire" if given the opportunity. There are several compelling reasons why he must acquire more people, money, and power. First, because work is the outlet the narcissistic manager has chosen as a buttress to his self-esteem, it is critical that he protect his job. By finding more power and importance in the organization, he makes himself indispensable to the company. Furthermore, gaining more power equals more control and more control allows the narcissistic manager to create the desired image of himself he wants to see in the organization. With more power, he has increased opportunity to hire and develop people who will agree with his point of view and carry out his ideas.

Another motive for building an empire is increasing his compensation (for more information on that, see Chapter 3). Most compensation systems are designed to pay more money to those with greater responsibilities. At the bottom of all this, the narcissistic manager builds an empire to conquer his fears and prove to himself that he is worthwhile.

Many a newcomer to the world of the narcissist has underestimated the protective instincts the narcissist has for his empire. The empire is, by definition, an extension of himself, and he can't allow it to be diminished. He does not give up without a serious fight.

SILENT SABOTAGE

Judy left her job at an upstart high tech company to take a better paying job with a public agency that had a long reputation for being a quintessential bureaucracy. Once Judy got her bearings in the organization, she discovered that a fellow director who also reported to her boss had, to put it mildly, a hybrid department. It was a hodgepodge of functions and jobs that the director had slowly and carefully accumulated over the years. There was no logic to the boundaries between Judy's department and her colleague's.

Judy suggested to her colleague that a reorganization might be more logical, not to mention more efficient. The suggestion ignited a storm of controversy, not the least of which was the passive withholding of all information to Judy's department. Time and time again she was silently sabotaged by her colleague. Eventually the colleague was successful at having Judy relocated to a site that was miles away from the corporate headquarters. Judy had most definitely underestimated the importance of boundaries and the vigor with which the narcissist protects his domain.

SEEKING VISIBILITY

Gaining high visibility within the company is critical to the narcissistic manager's fulfillment of his grand image. He pushes himself to achieve not merely for achievement's sake, but for the recognition and praise that accompanies that achievement. Without visibility, there can be no recognition.

DEMANDING VISIBILITY

John was a manufacturing manager for a large instrument and industrial equipment manufacturer that was acquired by a much larger national conglomerate. Because I was involved in the acquisition of the company, I had reviewed all of the management talent and knew of John's many accomplishments. John had a sterling reputation for dedication and hard work, having rocketed from an entry-level engineering position to director of materials management. John was well-liked and considered a talented manufacturing engineer. Despite his brief tenure in the management ranks, he had shown all the signs of being a successful senior manager.

Because much of the manufacturing equipment produced by John's company was purchased by high tech companies in and around the Silicon Valley area, the company had been located there for twenty years. During those years, the company had grown considerably, reaching sales of more than $20 million a year. Its customer base had grown, too, and now included companies from many different industries spread across the United States. Not surprisingly, a study looking at relocating the company to a more central and less expensive area was underway. After all, what was the point of paying the high rent and the higher competitive salaries of Silicon Valley when the company could function equally well in a less expensive location?

John was particularly interested in the idea of relocating. Coincidentally, both he and his wife were natives of Austin, Texas, the primary location being considered. To assist in the relocation, John had a member of his staff relocated to Austin to scope out the situation and report back to him. At the time of acquisition, the Austin relocation was looking like a done deal.

Shortly after the acquisition, the new parent company, also based in Silicon Valley, began to review the relocation plans. It seemed that a complete relocation to Austin would not be feasible because the parent company was intent on integrating its new acquisition. What would make a great deal of sense would be to relocate the manufacturing facility to an Austin plant that the parent company already owned. Under this plan, all manufacturing would relocate to Austin and John would head it up.

John seemed to go along with the plan at first, but over time his hesitancy became apparent. He began looking for other positions that might be available, perhaps even with the parent company, and voicing his concerns that he would be outside the mainstream in Austin. As the move date approached, he became very concerned. Austin had been a great idea when it meant the whole company was moving, but now it was looking more like a burial ground.

Just before the move date, John accepted another position with the research lab of the parent company. It was a move that offered no increase in salary and a significant decrease in responsibility. What was more important to John was that the position was highly visible and at the corporate headquarters. Despite the fact that moving to Austin meant a great deal to both himself and his family, the decreased visibility of that position posed too great a threat to his career.

What is important about John's decision is not whether he acted in the best interest of his career, but that his need for visibility dominated his decision. Other factors, like the wishes of his family or the opportunity for him to run a division, weren't given serious consideration. His fear of getting lost in the organization's political "outback" was paramount.

Like John, narcissistic managers demand visibility within the company. They understand the connection between visibility and recognition and know that without visibility there is little chance of promotion. What good is it to win the race if there is no one watching to applaud your victory?

BLAMING FAILURES ON OTHERS

The narcissistic manager never allows a failure to mar his reputation. If he can create a diversion or pin the failure on someone else, he avoids the career-limiting consequences that corporate failures can sometimes bring. If it's not his fault, then he can't be held responsible.

Diverting the Blame

I came face-to-face with the diversion of blame at a company where I worked several years ago. The company was located in the downtown of a large metropolitan area, and many of its employees commuted to work via public transportation. Although public transportation was a company-subsidized means of commuting (it eliminated the need for expensive parking garages), it did create a problem when site visits outside the immediate area were required. To solve this problem, the company maintained a fleet of cars available for any employee to use on company business. An employee would simply go to the basement of the building and check out whatever vehicle might be available.

The fleet cars were notorious lemons. They were in a serious state of disrepair, and you could never be sure if they would run. I once had to abandon a fleet car in a public parking lot because the motor didn't have enough power to pull out of a moderately inclined parking space! Another time I had to hold part of the dashboard off the floor so that a coworker could shift the car into gear. The final blow for me came when the fleet car I was driving stalled in the middle of a six-lane, five-mile-long bridge, causing another car to rear-end me and creating a backup for several miles.

When I returned to the office, I was livid. I was angered that the company risked my well-being to save a few bucks on auto repairs. After calming down, I wrote a polite memo to the manager in charge of the fleet cars informing him of the stalled car and ensuing accident. Thinking that I might be raising an important and urgent issue, I sent the memo over electronic mail.

Two days later I entered my office and found on my desk a lengthy computer report with many lines highlighted in yellow and a memo addressed to my vice-president from the manager of the fleet cars. The computer printout, I quickly discovered, was a listing of all of the fleet cars I had checked out over the past two years, and highlighted were the occasions when a car had been checked out to me overnight. The memo explained that I had excessive and unexplained overnight usage of the fleet cars and suggested that it might be personal use.

Needless to say, I was shocked. Since I taught regularly at the company's learning center, which was located some fifty miles away from the main office, it had indeed been my practice to check out a car the night before so that I could make the 8 a.m. session (rather than commuting to downtown, then checking out a car at 7 a.m. and, finally, driving to the learning center). But this was an issue beyond the rightness or wrongness of my use of the fleet cars. What did any of this have to do with the safety of the vehicles?

The manager of the fleet cars had diverted attention from my complaint by highlighting what he saw as my violation of company policy. While the one had nothing to do with the other, his response was effective in silencing my criticism, as I had to turn my attention to explaining my use of the fleet cars. I later learned that this manager had received several company awards for efficiency and had decreased fleet car expenditures dramatically during his time in the position. I suppose my complaint threatened to question his methods or was a threat to his procedure.

One powerful way of disowning a failure is to pin that failure on someone else and, if need be, even someone who works for you. It is the age-old use of a scapegoat; someone must bear the blame for transgressions. The narcissistic manager understands this well and has been known to offer others' careers as sacrifice instead of his own.

SCAPEGOATING

Ted was a programmer for one of the largest companies on the West Coast. He had worked for two years for a supervisor whose newly earned MBA was her self-proclaimed ticket to an executive position. She made it clear that her current position was only a stepping stone on her way to bigger things. Her agenda was to look as promotable as possible to her superiors and leave her current post in an otherwise dead-end department. The area she managed was writing a revision to the current inventory system of the bank that would change the entire workflow of the manufacturing divisions. Under much pressure to have the revision ready in time, she kept her staff moving ahead at all costs.

Much to her dismay, the programming hit a snag and, in a short time, fell hopelessly behind schedule. She needed a way to absolve herself of any direct responsibility for the delay, so she began a campaign to pin the blame on Ted. After several months of enduring her tyranny and "black listing," Ted realized the hopelessness of the situation and found a job at another company. Before leaving, however, he severely crippled the system by replacing random sections of code with faulty programs. It took the other programmers several months of work and testing to identify the offending statements and to fix the errors.

PSEUDO-CREATIVITY: BORROWED IDEAS

Of all the achievement techniques that the narcissistic manager uses, what I call *pseudo-creativity* is the most complex and effective at getting ahead. Pseudo-creativity is borrowing proven ideas from other organizations or people and implementing them as your own.

The narcissistic manager will massage borrowed ideas into his unmistakable style. By skirting the creative process and, consequently, the risk of trying out new ideas, he allows others to bear the risk of failure. He borrows their ideas only after proved successful. The pseudo-creative act begins with a visit to another company, attending a training program, or hiring a consultant to discover the path others have followed.

True creativity, on the other hand, wells from the self that is strong enough to give birth to original ideas. Sharing new, untried ideas makes one vulnerable to criticism and even rejection, which is not something those with weak self-esteem can tolerate. It takes fortitude and conviction to be confident enough in one's own ingenuity to propose an original idea and implement it in an organization. These are not the characteristics of the narcissistic manager.

Ironically, the narcissistic manager is frequently about the business of proposing new programs, products, and processes. He is never at a loss for suggestions. With a distinct preference for the flashy, he keeps his ear to the ground, always listening for the latest and greatest way of staying ahead.

The risk of criticism and failure stymies the narcissist's expression of truly creative ideas. The failure of an idea that he has personally authored cannot be easily diverted. He cannot blame anyone but himself for its failure. Because he derives so much of his self-esteem from his image, by admitting failure he would be forced to face personal inadequacies.

Protected Creativity

The narcissistic manager is not incapable, however, of some originality if he can completely control the outcome and evaluation of the creative effort. The scenario usually goes something like this: He dictates ideas to his staff and declares that the ideas will be carried out, providing no opportunity for criticism or staff participation. Since he knows that almost any idea can be made to look good given enough effort and money, he ensures that his ideas will not reflect badly upon himself by pouring the necessary resources into the project. His staff, having learned his intolerance of criticism, shields him by providing verbal support and praise. Thus, he minimizes the personal risk of creativity by creating a cocoon of protection for his idea.

WORKING FOR A NARCISSISTIC MANAGER

The personal cost of working for a narcissistic manager can be devastating for the unsuspecting employee. The anger and frustration that result from the manager's manipulative schemes can spill over into other business and personal relationships, destroying them as well. Beyond the anger, the quality of work life is devastated by the mistrust and demoralization created by the manager's narcissistic maneuverings. Without a doubt, those seeking satisfying and rewarding work are most likely to find it outside the employ of a narcissist.

My Tango With a Narcissist

I remember so well the frustration I felt when driving home from my first interview with Gene. I had gone to the interview, resumé in hand, ready to display all of my trophies of education and experience. After a few minutes of chatter about mutual acquaintances we had in graduate school (we had attended the same school), Gene began describing the job that was available. He was very precise with his words, something I appreciated and had rarely received from past supervisors, and spoke of exciting opportunities he and his staff would have to change the course of the company. He had joined the company only six months earlier and was certain that it had never been exposed to the brand of organizational development he espoused. He spoke at length of the role he would play both in the company at large and as the supervisor of the position for which I was being interviewed. He described his expectations of the position and asked me a few short questions, and on two occasions that I remember, interrupted my answer to complete it for me. That was the interview. I had been able to say very little about myself and my approach to the profession. I knew he had no idea of my capabilities. How could he? And yet, I felt that we had somehow related. He talked and I listened. Little did I know this would be the template for the rest of our relationship.

The final interviews for that position were with a variety of people from inside and outside the department. Two of the interviewers, Gene informed me, were on the interview schedule merely as a courtesy. The personnel department of the company required one interview with the company psychologist and one with a personnel manager. He confidentially informed me that their assessments would not be considered in the decision. These two individuals, I was to discover later, had expressed strong disagreement with Gene's approach on a previous project. In the typical black-and-white world of the narcissist, their opinions from that point forward were invalid in Gene's eyes. Those who do not support the cause of the narcissist are banished and silenced. Hence, their assessments of my potential were of no regard.

The Minefield

My first days on the job revealed the minefield I had walked into. For Gene, foes outnumbered friends by at least ten to one. Not all the animosity, however, had been of Gene's doing. Gene had been hired by a young and also newly hired vice president, Richard, who in the few months he had been with the company had managed to alienate just about everyone. Richard and Gene had worked together at another company and it was clear Gene was brought in as Richard's reinforcement. In a surprise overnight move, Richard had removed the prior incumbent of Gene's position while she was on vacation and had given it to Gene. Less than a year after that, to no one's surprise, corporate opinion turned against Richard, and he was fired.

Gene, on the other hand, did little to correct his now tenuous standing. He stampeded ahead with the political savvy of a zealot out to change the world. Gene had all the answers, and he expected his staff to carry them forward and implement them. Having little regard for what had been done before, Gene dismantled the existing programs and structure, completely reorganized the current staff, and began building the department he wanted.

It was clear to me that Gene's direct staff, including myself, had been chosen because of our willingness to subjugate our opinions and act on his wishes. While he never said it, we knew our jobs were to support his agenda and ensure the success of its implementation. Notwithstanding, it was always Gene's practice to ask each of our opinions in staff meeting. He would relinquish the floor and attentively listen to our comments, seemingly doing everything to encourage our opinions and participation. If one of us voiced a dissenting opinion, he would listen with all the more intensity. What would then follow was an excruciatingly long-winded response as to why we were mistaken, or perhaps a convoluted argument why we might think we disagree with him, but were actually in agreement on doing things his way. It became clear to me over the first months that Gene always listened attentively to criticism not for the value of its content, but to determine what and how long the argument against it should be. This, in Gene's mind, was what "open dialogue" was all about.

Gene's ultimate weapon proved to be his ability to dominate a conversation at length. Although he was not a particularly eloquent speaker, he was extremely bright. He always strategized his plan of attack before a meeting, making sure that any of his staff present in the meeting were aware of their duty to support his point of view. His strategy points were relatively simple: try to control the agenda, provide a compelling argument with convincing stories and visual aids and, if the opposition wasn't retreating, talk at length until the match was, at a minimum, declared a stalemate. More than one victory was won by exhausting the opponent.

Success Is Personal Achievement

Without question, Gene accomplished whatever objective he set out to achieve. On only a few occasions did I see him abandon his course of action and then only when it was made very clear that proceeding might jeopardize his employment. Over time I realized that even though Gene always claimed his projects were for the good of the company, he never seemed to choose a project that was low visibility or low budget. Without exception, his choices always favored the flashy, high-dollar types of programs that often attract lots of executive attention. Gene measured success not in profit and loss, but in the economies of personal achievement and glory.

During my first days on the job, Gene reviewed each of my staff member's files with me. His closing comments of that discussion stayed in my memory for some time afterwards: "I'm sure by the same time next year, you'll have a completely new staff." Nothing more had to be said. My first job would be to clean house, *his* house.

MOVING THE THREAT TO THE SIDELINES

What I discovered in the next days about my staff, and two members in particular, was that they had been publicly critical of Gene. One member, Lance, was part-time and had worked in the department for six years. Lance, independent and vocal, was well-liked and had become the personal confidant of a number of directors and, as far as I knew, at least one vice president. Working closely with the distribution side of the business, he had been extremely successful at helping the management team turn around an otherwise failing business unit.

I believe that Lance's strong political connections in the organization were what started his trouble with Gene. Gene was troubled by Lance's influence in the inner sanctum of the executive suite; this was influence Gene couldn't control. The first time Lance disagreed with Gene and refused to use his connections to implement one of Gene's many programs, Gene shut him off. Lance's informal power in the organization was far too threatening for Gene.

From that day forward, Gene refused to see any value in what Lance had accomplished. He did his best to denigrate Lance whenever the opportunity arose—a tactic that eventually reflected badly on Gene. When Lance refused to go away quietly, Gene proposed radical changes to Lance's job and to the services he provided the distribution business, in essence making Lance a sideline player in the business.

In the year that Lance remained with the company following my hiring, I was under increasing pressure to make Lance a full-time employee. My staffing needs were tight to begin with, but every request I made for additional headcount was met with a discussion of Lance's part-time status. Gene and I both knew there were compelling medical reasons why Lance could not work full time, but Gene refused to discuss it. Business was business; I needed more staff so I should require Lance to work full-time. Eventually the pressure and tension became so painful that Lance resigned from the company.

Not only had Lance contributed significantly to the company in the past; he had displayed professional skills that had been recognized at the highest levels of the company. It was unfortunate that he had committed the fatal error of criticizing Gene. From that point on, Lance could do nothing right in Gene's eyes, and it was only a matter of time before he stopped trying.

The Grand Slipcover

A showman at heart, Gene had an affinity for the spotlight. If something could be printed on glossy paper stock or in some way be connected to a high tech device, it was always a sure winner. Often I learned that I could get both his approval and budget dollars for the projects with pizzazz. The most profound instance involved a week-long entry-level management training program that, when the final tally was in, had cost $200,000 for us to develop, one third of which had gone to produce a three-minute multimedia presentation to open and close the program! Upbeat music was written especially for the video, which included an aerial shot of dozens of employees (actors) running with jubilance on the roof of the company headquarters. It was quite an eye-catcher.

Gene had us show that video to every executive and middle manager who would sit to watch it. And watch it they did, in a new training room Gene had built that was equipped with the latest in rear projection and sound equipment.

Placing a carefully crafted slipcover over reality was one of Gene's strongest skills. No matter how a project turned out, its outcome was molded into something that echoed his agenda. Once, shortly after the introduction of a major company campaign for improving customer service, Gene retained the services of one of the best employment testing firms in the country to run a pilot study of a new customer service test they had developed. At the conclusion of the pilot study, the results showed that the new test would improve upon the existing company employment test by only a few percentage points. Although the new test would nearly double the company's testing costs and showed a dubious increase in probability of selecting good sales associates, Gene declared the pilot a success and moved full-steam ahead in implementing the test. The chance for him to make it known that his department was now testing every company job applicant for customer service was far more delicious than the reality that the new test would make little if any difference in the company's hiring decisions.

Gene honestly believed his way was the best for the company. Although it is true that his way was also best for him and his career, he would certainly assert that those personal benefits were the legitimate accompaniments to success. Undoubtedly he felt the expansion of his power base in the company and the furthering of his career were the direct result of his good management and leadership and were rightful rewards for a job well done. Like most narcissistic managers, Gene's self-image was merged with his job, and he could not understand the subtle difference between actions motivated by his desire to propel his career forward and those that would benefit the company. Indeed, while the differences may have appeared slight, the impact was prodigious.

Gene's management style started a slow leak that eventually robbed every ounce of innovative spirit and passion from the staff. A long-time member of Gene's staff explained it as "draw the star" (a training exercise often used with managers). Everyone who draws a star draws it in a slightly different way: No two are exactly alike. The staff member described working for Gene as the never-ending task of trying to mimic the star Gene had drawn in his head. You would present your idea to Gene on whatever project or task it was that he had assigned you and he would then discuss your idea, subtly dropping hints at how he would do it. Your job was then to come back with a star that matched his star. The closer the approximation, the greater likelihood that your star would win the prize of his approval. A master of manipulation, Gene played this game to provide a thinly veiled illusion that the idea was really your own. There was little point in pursuing ideas disparate from Gene's, as he would throw up road blocks at every juncture. By his design, his was the path of least resistance.

I will never forget the experience of working for Gene. Just knowing that I was pushing myself harder than I ever had to make him look more successful left me cold. I saw my staff and colleagues' motivations begin to falter as they too began to realize that they were only being used by a manager who cared little for their welfare and the welfare of the company. Over time I saw what was once a hard-working and committed group of people disintegrate into something resembling drones enduring their daily chores. Overall commitment to quality and customer service fell as we were reduced to non-thinking cogs in the machine Gene was building.

WORKING FOR A NARCISSIST

People handle the experience of working for a narcissistic manager in different ways. Those who have experienced a narcissistic parent or worked for another narcissist are less likely to react in extreme ways, as they are no stranger to his tactics and self-aggrandizing. Others who are more independent of thought or more passionate about their trade than they are of corporate politics have the most difficult time adjusting to the demands of the narcissistic manager and usually find ways of avoiding or protecting themselves from him. And, of course, the most explosive combination is one narcissist working for another. A collision of determination and ego, one will not survive the other. You can bet that over time, one will destroy the other.

Getting on the Glory Train

Because the narcissistic manager is on a self-made train to glory, some may see an opportunity to hook up for the ride. Her history of winning the biggest and best projects attracts those who are looking for their fair share of the glory. Because she has a history of success and accomplishments, the invitation to work for her can be quite alluring. Make no mistake: Having an energetic and enthusiastic manager on your side who is fighting for resources can be a big boost to your career and allow you to accomplish things that would have otherwise been impossible.

The fast-paced excitement of working with a narcissistic manager can be very attractive. For some, the simple change from a job that is routine and monotonous to the competitive and confrontational environment she fosters is what attracts them. Because she often works quickly to build her empire, working for her is filled with constant change, and even though it entails control and manipulation, it may be inherently more interesting than the available alternatives. In any event, it is quite possible for employees to use the narcissist for their needs, just as she uses them to fulfill her own.

Colliding Head-On

Another scenario that almost everyone who has worked with a narcissistic manager experiences at some point is the "head-on collision." Because he is determined and generally inflexible, the narcissist will eventually have some conflict with those with whom he works. Conflict provides the narcissistic manager with an opportunity to prove the rightness of his stance. The more opposition he meets, the more he entrenches in his ideas and the more important it becomes for him to win. Sadly, any merit in the opposing idea is undoubtedly lost in the frenzy to achieve victory, and his employees eventually learn that the cost in time and effort isn't worth the confrontation. It is simply easier to do things his way.

The narcissistic manager has an advantage in dealing with conflicts in that he isn't threatened by the possibility of having to confront others with what he sees as their mistakes, or to disagree with them. While most of us are uncomfortable with forcing an issue, he draws comfort and confidence from his extensive experience in coercing others. He has learned over the years that he can gain much by simply pushing a little further than most others are willing to push. Indeed, experience has taught him that if he pushes hard enough, he usually gets what he wants.

In the same vein, the narcissist in power counts on the fact that others will be uncomfortable with confrontation and uses that to his advantage. He may actually create situations in which others feel intimidated and would be less likely to challenge him. For example, he knows that if he announces his favorite, new, and not-yet-approved program in a certain large meeting, no one is likely to speak up and challenge him. He uses his aggressive stance to intimidate his staff and deter them from challenging him in return. After all, no matter what their argument, he will always win by, if nothing else, pulling rank. When they privately challenge him, he may escalate the disagreement quickly to a level at which his opponent is uncomfortable and retreats.

Compliance

What most employees of a narcissistic manager eventually settle into is passive compliance. They realize that if they take his ideas and implement them, life becomes much easier. Rather than trying to swim upstream, experience tells the employees that the downstream path is easier and much faster. If they are successful in opposing him, he discounts the success for whatever reasons are handy, and if they have the misfortune of failing, the employees bear the brunt of his blame and punishment. When they do a project his way, they cannot fail; for no matter what the outcome, he will declare it a success.

When faced with his domination of an issue, the narcissistic manager can honestly say that no one spoke up to disagree. Even when given the opportunity to disagree, his employees know all too well the consequences of challenging him and will remain silent. In fact, if those employees choose to take a contrary path, they know it is better not to raise the issue at all and avoid his involvement than to raise the issue and run the risk of opposing him. The simple fact is that he can't dominate what he doesn't know.

Resentment and Anger

One of the phases that employees who work for a narcissistic manager may face is colored with resentment and anger. Nobody likes to be manipulated. Not only does manipulation generate anger toward the person doing the manipulation; it breeds self-anger in the victim for allowing the manipulation. Because the narcissistic manager often acts without regard to the impact he is having on the lives of others, he can easily carry through plans that may devastate the careers of others. When an employee discovers that she has been used for his purposes to the detriment of her own needs and career, this realization can generate a passionate resistance to ever participating in his schemes again.

Resistance to the narcissistic manager can come in many forms. His direct staff learns to express their resistance in more covert and passive ways, careful to avoid his watchful eye. Such resistance might come in the form of alerting others to the narcissistic manager's ulterior motives or leaking damaging information to other departments. As in the example of the programmer who destroyed a company system, it can come in the form of grand sabotage. Because the manager will not allow his staff to directly express their feelings, they exhibit their anger in more covert ways.

In many ways the narcissistic manager is on a high wire to success without a net. The ire and ill will he creates with others effects a tension-filled environment in which they have to perform. Should they trip and waver, there are many who are waiting to swoop in and devour. The angry mob is waiting for a legitimate invitation to focus its anger on its target. The narcissistic manager can go from being on the top of success to being unemployed in a very short time.

Quit and Stay

The final phase that those who work for a narcissistic manager go through is one of "checking out." Once they realize that confrontation doesn't work and that anger and resentment takes an enormous amount of energy, they settle into a state of apathy. They mentally leave their brain outside of any work-related activity and make calculated guesses as to how long they can continue before being fired. While this phase is most commonly measured in months before they move on, I have seen employees who have stayed in it for years. They simply don't care. Whatever they have coming to them, whether it is sick leave, vacation, or an expense account, they exploit to policy limits. They work only the required hours and produce just enough to fend off their own boredom. They simply disengage themselves from a situation in which they feel powerless.

The Enablers

One type of person often works successfully (for a time) with a narcissist. Borrowing a term from the self-help codependency literature, I call such people corporate enablers. Their own past experiences mold them to fit well into a working relationship with a narcissist.

Enablers are extremely important to the success of the narcissist. In fact, the grand world of the narcissist would collapse if it weren't for the applauding audience of enablers. The enablers are all those who complement the ways of the narcissist: They are his mirror, his accomplice, his straight man. Enablers are the catalysts that create a narcissistic reality in the organization.

Most enablers have no intention of doing harm. They are committed, hard-working, and very loyal employees who are willing to give everything they have in exchange for the security that comes from winning the approval of an authority figure. Enablers crave security, and, unlike the narcissist, have little need for power. Instead, a burning need for protection drives them forward. At the extreme, enablers are willing to sacrifice their own reputations and careers in exchange for the protective embrace of an authority figure.

When an enabler and a narcissist meet, the attraction is powerful and magnetic. The narcissist desperately seeks others to help him prop his fragile grand facade, and the enabler seeks the opportunity to prove his worth to someone he deems more important and powerful than himself. The narcissist and enabler are like two pieces of a puzzle perfectly matched. Their needs are carved as mirror images which, once drawn together, create a powerful bond.

The enabler gives over his power to the narcissist. He becomes a junky for the narcissist's praise and will do whatever is necessary to stay in the security of his good graces. He will give beyond healthy limits and endure unconscionable abuse at the hands of the narcissist. The narcissist leverages this vulnerability and uses the enabler to accomplish his self-serving goals.

The enabler, much like the narcissist, is a person who is caught in the endless cycle of proving his self-worth. Early life experiences taught him there is danger when others assess him as a failure. The beast of anxiety is constantly nipping at his heels, pushing him faster and harder to earn the grade and ward off the danger he imagines is on the other side of success.

Here lies the difference and similarity between the narcissist and enabler: Both are driven to win the approval of others—the enabler by a fear of failure and the narcissist by the frustration of thwarted entitlement. The narcissist demands recognition and power. The enabler ingratiates himself to those whose approval he desires. The narcissist hungers after

power while the enabler seeks the shelter offered by the protective shadow of the powerful.

Usually the child of highly critical parents, the adult enabler has internalized those parental criticisms. No matter
what he does, he can never please the voices that play and
replay in his head. His work is never good enough.

The only reprieve the enabler gets from his internal task-
master comes from the approval of a surrogate parent. The
surrogate parent—a boss, respected coworker, mentor—can
impart temporary feelings of self-worth that the enabler cannot give to himself. When the surrogate parent approves of
him he can, for a short time, silence the tormenting and painful voices.

Unfortunately, the enabler quickly loses the boost of self-
confidence that comes from the narcissist's contingent praise,
discounts his own accomplishments, and sets out on a new
hunt for proof that he is really worthwhile. Like the narcissist,
the enabler's needs are rooted in his earliest childhood experiences; despite his best efforts to fill those nagging needs, they
are endless in their demands upon him. The enabler uncon-
sciously thinks he can once and for all fulfill these needs if he
can prove himself worthy. Unfortunately, a lifetime of proof
never solves the problem.

As a result of years of security-seeking behavior, the enabler becomes quite adept at perceiving the needs of those
around him. If he is to win their approval, he must first discover what it is they want. Before he can form an opinion, take
a stand, or reveal himself, he must first determine what is
required of him. Then, like a chameleon, he fashions himself
to suit his environment.

Like the narcissist, the enabler is often mistaken as the
perfect corporate citizen. His words are quotes from the latest
corporate dogma. His opinions are aligned with the current
corporate strategy. He is the champion of the corporate status
quo.

To a company outsider, the enabler can sound like he
speaks another language. For example, I once visited an enabler in a company with which I had never worked before.
While explaining the company strategy, the enabler kept re-

ferring to his company as a "value-added retailer." He used the term forcefully and often, not realizing that I didn't have clue as to what he was talking about. I wondered how any retailer could stay in business if it wasn't adding value. Wasn't the very definition of any business to "add value" in some form? As it turns out, "value-added" was a term his boss had recently used to describe a new change in company pricing. The enabler had quickly adopted his boss's jargon without considering what it precisely meant. He had retreated into the safety of the corporate-sanctioned verbiage.

Enabler and Narcissist

The enabler and narcissist form a coalition that is centered on fulfilling the narcissist's personal image of success. The narcissist sets the strategy and agenda, while the enabler works tirelessly to accomplish it. The enabler makes the narcissist look good, always withholds criticism, and protects the narcissist from others in the organization who would encroach on the narcissist's territory. The enabler helps the narcissist expand his power base and, when necessary, performs reconnaissance to maintain such a corporate fiefdom. At times, enablers have been known to sabotage other areas of the company just to make the narcissist look successful.

The narcissist is dependent on the actions of the enabler but never succumbs to this dependency. He always takes the upper hand in the relationship, using the enabler to get what he wants while promising the enabler protection. Should the enabler become useless—or worse, a liability—the narcissist will sever the relationship and toss him aside, perhaps even using the enabler as a scapegoat to deflect his own culpability. While the narcissist uses the enabler and feigns loyalty and affection, in reality the enabler is nothing more to the narcissist than a stepping stone.

Enablers eventually discover this very painful truth. The disappointment and loss they feel only confirm their deep-seated fears that their inadequacy somehow destroyed the relationship. As time progresses, they find themselves repeatedly attracted to, used, and discarded by aspiring narcissists. Their anger and resentment grows.

This is the dark side of an enabler. Outwardly, he is loyal to the narcissist, but inside he is vibrating with anger. He resents his dependency upon the narcissist's approval. He despises the manipulations. On some level he realizes that his sacrifice and tremendous effort mean little to the narcissist.

What keeps the enabler from exploding is his fear of his own anger. Anger was not a valid emotion in his childhood, and he fears it as an adult. Anger is dangerous, and its expression can separate him from his source of security. Anger is something to be swallowed, repressed, and denied. The enabler is convinced that nothing good can come from its expression.

In true Freudian fashion, the enabler's resentment eventually seeps out. Tragically, he secretly despises the person whose approval he desperately needs. In private, the enabler spills this resentment and spreads an infectious misery to those with whom he works, all the time continuing to fulfill the wishes of the narcissist.

The Enabler's Burnout

The problem of enabler burnout and demoralization is endemic in today's corporate environment. The gradual rise and celebration of narcissism in some organizations has left a trail of hard-working but discarded enablers in its wake. I believe the palpable demise of employee morale is directly related to enabler burnout.

The following are selected portions of an interview with a career-long enabler. The interviewee is in his late fifties and personally holds twelve patents on industry-related technology. The transcript is exact except for a few small changes to protect the interviewee's identity.

> I'm tired. I have to admit it. You get tired of the intense stupidity around here. It's been a long time. Oh there've been some good things—a few really

bright guys I had the pleasure of working for—but the fact is I should have gotten out long ago. Now it's too late—there're the mortgage payments and children in college and I'm not sure where else I could get this kind of income.

I guess what I object to most is the wastage of people around here—myself included. I've been passed over twice now so I guess you can say I'm bitter about that, and it's true I am. But as I look back at even the good times I realize that my talent and all my hard work was used by a parade of up-and-comers. Sure, they told me I was part of the team and all that, but when the time came for promotions, they always took the credit. I can say without any hesitation that I am personally responsible for the careers of half a dozen executives around here.

I suppose I could have played the game too, but I never had the stomach for corporate politics. Some new guy would be brought in and he would announce a new research program of some sort. The rest of us would go to work, sometimes night and day, to keep his promises. When we would deliver all that he had promised, he was promoted and we were forgotten.

I can't tell you how many new managers I've broken in. They would come into R&D without a clue as to what we do here. I'd spend weeks giving them a crash course on the state of the art and then the next thing I knew they were marching my ideas in front of the executive committee just like they were their own.

The truth is, I don't think upper management cares about who comes up with the ideas or who did all the work. All they care about are results. If a manager can produce results—no matter what they have to do to get those results—their career is as good as gold.

Here's another interview with a recently laid off enabler:

> Now that I look back on it, I realize that my biggest mistake was aligning myself so closely with Mike. When I came to work for Mike, he told me that he was going to make some dramatic changes around here and that I should steer clear of the "old timers." Over the next two years, he and I worked together to turn the department around, and we did it, but not without making a few enemies along the way. . . .
>
> Mike ended up replacing almost all of the staff with the exception of myself and one other senior specialist. Everyone else had to go. He'd either make their lives so miserable that they would come in one day and quit or he'd fire them.
>
> For the four years I worked for Mike I was his right hand man. We worked together on everything. . . . Every year my IPM [company's performance review] was the best—just shy of walking on water. Those were my best years with the company.
>
> Upper management seemed really pleased with what Mike was doing. A lot of the seventeenth floor [the company's executive suite] thought the department was long due for an overhaul. All the same, a lot of people in the company were angry about the changes. They didn't understand what Mike and I were doing and they were holding on to the past. Friendships run deep with the lifers around here.
>
> That's what I didn't expect. When Mike got his promotion to Nuclear [another company division headquartered in another state] I was left dangling in the wind. The same day that Mike's replacement took over—another lifer—people started treating me differently. All my projects were taken away and I was left with nothing to do. In two months, I was laid off.
>
> Before I got the ax I called Mike to see if he

could pull some strings on my behalf. He acted pretty distant on the phone and told me there was nothing he could do.

Much like the narcissist, the enabler first appears to be the ideal employee. In time, however, the enabler becomes a serious problem for the organization. The misery and frustrations of enablers become infectious and drag down the morale of the organization. They can quickly depress the work environment.

The narcissist and enabler form a coalition that is hard to beat. Most narcissistic leaders would falter quickly without the support and protection of enabling troops. By enlisting loyal enablers, the narcissist can establish territorial power and, if necessary, dispatch reinforcements to protect his boundaries. Together, the narcissist and enabler construct an empire that creates unnecessary waste and conflict within the organization.

Section 2

NARCISSISM IN THE ORGANIZATION

The Narcissistic Organization

Narcissism invades the organization one executive at a time. If one narcissist is allowed to rise to power, he inevitably hires reinforcements. Slowly, critical power positions are filled with those who will support his agenda. Some of these are themselves narcissists; others fill the supporting role of the enabler (Chapter 2). One narcissist can create a cluster of narcissism that, if unchecked, can grow to dominate an entire organization.

Typically, the narcissistic organization consists of a few powerful narcissists who control the corporate agenda. Narcissistic leaders set in motion a corporate environment that is purely survival of the fittest. These top executives take pride in watching their junior counterparts compete with one another and are quick to reward the one who emerges as the victor. Rather than promoting the executive who acts most responsibly in the corporate interest, they anoint the emergent political victor. Surviving the political infighting is seen as a rite of passage to the executive suite of the narcissistic organization.

Very quickly, the rest of the onlooking organization learns how to behave. The rules of the narcissistic organization are surprisingly simple and straightforward: Always look good and do anything you can to make your boss look good; take as much for yourself as you can; constantly watch your back, and, in the end, remember that results are all that really matter.

Financially troubled organizations are particularly susceptible hosts for narcissism. The narcissist's singular focus on image and the associated obsession with profit are tempting to organizations that are struggling for financial stability. The narcissist's unswerving willingness to cut costs may be just what the organization needs for survival.

There can be no doubt that some narcissistic management practices have turned around more than a few faltering companies. The commanding, take-charge management style and the obsessive focus on winning can be a significant force in redirecting the corporate strategy. The most successful narcissists often promote themselves as "turn around" specialists.

The problem of narcissism in the organization, however, emerges after the stopgap measures have taken effect. In the process of dramatically stripping the organization of the "fat," the narcissist also strips away such essential factors as organizational mission, values, and employee loyalty.

LOST MISSION

Of all the effects of a narcissist on an organization, the destruction of corporate mission is the most damaging. Corporate mission is the reason the organization is in business. Ultimately, mission defines the universe of products and services offered by a company.

But mission is much more than just a definition of the company; it is a conviction—a unifying purpose. Without a mission, the company is reduced to nothing more than a balance sheet. Corporate mission is the source of inspiration that motivates employees to excellence. Mission is the power that transforms employees from mere hired hands to caring stewards of the company.

I once heard mission adeptly described in more personal

terms: "If you worked for free, mission is the reason why you would work for the company."

For long-term employees and managers, corporate mission takes on just such a personal significance. It is the moral justification for spending one's career working for a particular company and a source of personal pride and conviction. It is a focus for collaboration and a strong motivator.

The narcissistic organization dilutes corporate mission to oblivion. Material success, not mission, becomes the only value of consequence. Management decisions hinge solely on financial returns without regard to the impact of those decisions on other values.

Once mission is stripped away, the only reason for corporate existence is to pay a dividend to shareholders. Employees, unable to find inspiration and meaning for their jobs, are reduced to mere wage earners. Besides satiating consumption needs, their jobs provide little motivation to excel.

This is the death of the corporate soul. There is no passion beyond greed. Collaboration is abandoned for individual competition. Loyalty to customers withers and dies. Employees become disposable.

ORGANIZATIONAL STRUCTURE

Since there is no clear mission for the narcissistic organization, its structure begins to evolve around personalities rather than work functions or products. Not surprisingly, the structure almost always acquires a totalitarian element where one person single-handedly runs the organization (or organizational unit). All others beneath this manager are merely supporting members of the staff. Sometimes there is one narcissistic leader at the top who runs the entire organization; other times, especially in very large corporations, there are several narcissistic leaders who completely control their territorial "empire" within the larger organization.

Narcissistic companies tend to grow haphazardly, with little apparent logic. The organization chart grows according to the borders of power rather than business necessity. The corporate expansion strategy is more like corporate gerrymandering: Growth comes in areas that expand the power and control of the narcissistic leader.

The "organic" structure evolves as the narcissistic manager expands his territory and then organizes it for maximum control. He may place very diverse functions under the oversight of a trusted lieutenant simply because he knows that manager will carefully execute his plan. Other, seemingly important organizational units may be disbanded to reduce the power of an internal revival or to punish an insolent subordinate supervisor. The organization is the narcissist's chessboard, and he arranges all of the pieces so that he is in the best possible position.

FIGHTING CHANGE

One of the more curious aspects of the narcissistic organization is its resistance to change. Narcissists, as I have previously noted, spend a great deal of time strategizing their moves and arranging those around them to support their power domain. As a result, they are very resistant to any change that encroaches upon the power structures they have built. They will sabotage any move that threatens their position.

A favorite tactic of the narcissist is to "hijack" an organizational change program. By placing himself in a position to control the change, he can protect his power base and, if he is lucky, expand his domain and his organizational visibility. In Chapter 6, I take an in-depth look at how a narcissistic leader derails a change effort by refocusing it in his best interest.

IDOLIZED LEADERS

Narcissistic leaders normally seek and attract subordinates who are politically nonthreatening and somewhat dependent. The narcissistic leader's action-oriented, grandiose style well suits the dependency needs of such people, permitting them to take up major responsibilities for the organization while subordinating their own needs to those of the leader. Of course, we all have dependency needs, but individuals attracted to narcissistic leaders have more than most.

Subordinates of narcissistic executives tend to idealize their charismatic leaders, ignoring their faults and exaggerating their strengths. This idealization may derive from subordinates' feelings of unworthiness. They are therefore unduly flattered even by off-the-cuff remarks of praise from the leader, and devastated by the mildest reprimands. A narcissistic leader's subordinates thus permit the executive to wield an excessive amount of control over them through psychological manipulation.

In the narcissistic culture, whole worlds revolve around the leader. The hopes and ambitions of other managers in the company center on their idealized top executive. The dreams and desires of these narcissistic leaders become the goals and operating plans of the followers with an almost mystical fervor. The leader's very presence can bolster employee initiative and increase morale.

CENTRALIZED POWER

Strategists make decisions based on the understood preferences of the narcissistic leaders, skirting facts and detailed analyses, and ignoring both market changes and consumer demands. They address widely disparate projects in random fashion. Power is centralized, preserving the top executive's prerogative to initiate bold ventures independent of anyone else's stabilizing options.

A major weakness is the relationships narcissistic executives have with their employees. Their grandiose designs rarely leave room for much consultation with, or feedback from, the second-tier managers. One manager, for instance, insisted on "immersion management" and personally dissected even the most minor details of matters perhaps better attended to by subordinate experts. Participative decision-making was something he never encouraged nor expected could substantially help; he habitually refused feedback. The inadequate role of second-tier managers in a narcissistic organization means vital information may never reach the CEO; capable managers will be driven away by frustration and their places will be taken by uncreative yes-men.

CLOSED SYSTEM

The narcissistic organization becomes a closed system that exists to fulfill the objectives of its leaders. External changes in markets and customer needs have increasingly less impact on this organization. The company spins in a seemingly independent orbit; the leader creates a reason for being and the subordinates work to fulfill that meaning.

SYTHESIZING A FANTASY

Maryann Keller describes just this kind of organization in her 1989 book, *Rude Awakening: The Rise, Fall and Struggle for Recovery of General Motors*. Describing then-chairman Roger Smith:

"For thirty-one years, Smith moved up through the ranks of GM as the consummate corporate player—the GM culture coursed in his veins. Admiration for and loyalty to the organization was at the core of his being. He was one of a new breed of corporate politicians whose success depended on their ease in wearing the corporate mantle. Translated, that meant, 'Above all, be loyal to your superior's agenda.' "[1]

John De Lorean, former head of the Chevrolet division and GM's one-time "golden boy," writes of the increasing isolation of GM executives from the real issues of business:

"This system quickly shut top management off from the real world because it surrounded itself in many cases with 'yes' men. There soon become no real vehicle for adequate outside input. Lower executives, eager to please the boss and rise up the corporate ladder, worked hard to learn what he wanted or how he thought on a particular subject. They then either fed the boss exactly what he wanted to know, or they modified their own proposals to suit his preferences.

"Original ideas were often sacrificed in deference to what the boss wanted. Committee meetings no longer were forums for open discourse, but rather either soliloquies by the top man, or conversations between a few top men with the rest of the meeting looking on. In Fourteenth Floor meetings, often only three people, Cole, Gerstenberg, and Murphy would have anything substantial to say, even though there were fourteen or fifteen executives present. The rest of the team would remain silent, speaking only when spoken to. When they did offer a comment, in many cases it was just to paraphrase what had already been said by one of the top guys."[2]

It is a collusion where individuals who are retained and promoted are those who know how things are supposed to look, according to the ideology of the dominant coalition. Reality has increasingly limited impact on executive decision making, and those who succeed are those who can synthesize a fantasy that is more to the liking of the narcissistic leaders.

CLOSED TO BAD NEWS

CompuLease Corporation (not its real name) is another clear example of how the narcissistic organization can become an impenetrably closed system—especially to bad news. CompuLease is a Massachusetts leasing company formed in the late 1960s by Max Shaw. The company has been boldly engaged in the risky business of leasing business computers, expensive machine tools, boilers, airplanes, and anything else Shaw and his staff could get their hands on. Concentrating on small- and medium-sized clients and undercutting other leasing firms by wide margins, CompuLease grew to $1.1 billion in revenue in its first dozen years.

By 1979 the company seemed to be facing a highly promising future.

But in the same year, CompuLease's stock took an unexpected beating, plunging eighteen points in the first quarter. In the second quarter, $60 million in losses forced Shaw to resign. Warnings had been there for over a year, but Shaw had chosen not to heed them. CompuLease's computer orders had already begun to fall sharply months before, the result of speculation that a major competitor was about to offer more competitive products. Shaw, however, decided the order drop had more to do with CompuLease's internal problems and forged ahead, confident that the leasing orders would quickly pick up. One colleague remembers Shaw's habit of closing his ears to bad news, enforcing a top-down, limited-information communication system. Thus, even when information was gathered by lower-level managers, such managers would usually have too little influence on organizational decisions to permit their knowledge to make any difference.

The company's performance goals, for example, often seemed arbitrary, unrealistic, and determined by fiat. As another CompuLease official explained, "When we got to a planning session with our calculators, we were told to punch in a 35 percent increase over last year. There was no appeal. My boss just sat there and said, 'Max needs so many millions from you.' "

CompuLease's story is one familiar to many narcissistic organizations. The company grew much too rapidly for its initial control system to remain effective. Shaw's impulsive acquisitions caused operating problems that took too long to spot, and rapid diversification intensified the firm's already poor internal communications system. By 1979, cost control at CompuLease had totally broken down. For the first time since its founding, CompuLease showed overall losses for the entire year. Twenty-five percent of its 6,400 employees had to be laid off, and eighteen of its thirty-two divisions were discontinued. Shaw's exclusive reliance on his intuition had proved inadequate. CompuLease was caught off guard by the competitor's new series, and Shaw's grandiosity may have been partially to blame. CompuLease's organization had proved too weak too support Shaw's narcissistic style of management. It took until September 1983 before CompuLease finally emerged from Chapter 11 bankruptcy.

KILLING THE MESSENGER

The narcissistic organization rarely handles criticism constructively. Instead, it chooses to manipulate feedback to suit its own purposes. Some of the tactics used include putting a positive spin on news that is otherwise negative, inventing contradicting experts and evidence, and attacking the critic.

Respected management philosopher Peter Drucker found himself the target of a vigorous attack after he criticized General Motors. A Harvard professor at the time, Drucker published *The Concept of a Corporation*, which dissected the structure of GM. While the public regarded the work as decidedly pro-business and favorable to GM, the leadership of GM viewed it as criticism and denounced the book and its author openly.

When Ralph Nader published his 1965 book about the Corvair, *Unsafe at Any Speed*, GM hired private detectives to dig up personal smut on Nader in an attempt to discredit him. Despite the fact that GM's own engineers had declared the Corvair unsafe and the company's legal department was overrun with lawsuits regarding Corvair related injuries and deaths, Nader had dared to attack the organization. He had become an enemy of the corporation, and he had to be stopped.[3]

One blatant example of a company trying to obscure serious internal problems occurred in 1995 when Archer Daniels Midland Co. (ADM) fired executive Mark Whitacre after learning that he had been a government informant on price fixing at the company for more than two years. One year after the firing and a publicized investigation by the justice department, ADM sued Whitacre for $30 million, claiming that he broke a signed confidentiality agreement when he told the government about scandal. Whitacre denies having signed the agreement and notes: "They're saying my responsibility was to the company, not the government." Rather than focus on cleaning up the unsavory business practices, ADM chose to detract attention from the wrongdoing and discredit the source of the criticism.

On October 17, 1996, ADM CEO Dwayne Andreas apologized to shareholders and announced that ADM was paying the federal government a $100 million fine for price fixing. In addition, the 78-year-old Andreas, revealed that ADM was cooperating with the government's investigation of two ADM executives, one of which is Andreas's only son and heir apparent, Michael D. "Mick" Andreas. At the time of this writing, ADM is continuing with its suit against Whitacre.

With the recent growth of narcissistic organizations, several large-scale trends have emerged as the result of changing business practices and ethics. Two trends, excessive executive compensation and widespread layoffs, have now become fixtures on the corporate scene.

A Passion for Greed

If anything is sacred to the narcissistic organization, it is greed. No other business trend of recent times reflects this better than the unprecedented rise in executive salaries. As the number of narcissistic organizations increases, the discrepancy in pay between senior executives and the average employee has reached hundred-fold portions. Executives who are so passionate about cutting costs, it seems, are even more passionate about their own paychecks.

In 1980, the average CEO's paycheck was $624,996—42 times the pay of the average worker. By 1996, however, that gap had risen by a multiplier of 141, as the average top boss took home $3.7 million in total compensation. Between 1995 and 1996 the average CEO's pay rose a generous 30 percent while the average white collar worker only saw a 4.2 percent raise.

As shocking as these numbers may be, senior executives are reaping even greater rewards in long-term stock options. For example, in 1994 Lawrence Bossidy, chairman of Allied-Signal, received a ten-year stock option on 1.8 million shares of AlliedSignal stock. If the stock rises 10 percent annually over the ten-year span of the option, Bossidy will gain $100.5 million on stock grants alone, making his annual compensation of $12 million look rather meager.

Executive stock options have risen dramatically in recent years. Because this form of compensation is often less visible and carries certain tax advantages, many companies have increased the size and number of options granted to executives. In the 1970s, most companies would reserve about 3 percent of their outstanding stock as options for management. Today, the 200 largest companies set aside nearly 10 percent of their stock for top executives. According to a one recent survey, fifty-five of the nation's top executives are sitting on options worth $10 million or more.

The skyrocketing pay seems to be, in large part, a self-perpetuating climb where one executive's excesses are used to justify another's. Take, for example, the response of Allied-Signal's compensation committee in defense of the hefty payouts to Bossidy: "[the pay contract] is competitive with compensation packages currently offered to the nation's most highly regarded, sought-after executives."

Sharing the Pain?

In true narcissistic fashion, the idea that senior executives should "share the pain" of their cost cutting efforts is not a popular one in executive boardrooms. When AT&T's Chairman Robert Allen laid off 40,000 workers, he was awarded a stock option package that increased his compensation by 143 percent to $15.9 million. The same thing happened at United Technologies when Chairman Robert Daniell pulled in $11.2 million in pay after six years of vicious cost-cutting that resulted in layoffs of 30,000 employees. Frank Shrontz, CEO of

Boeing Co., took in a 75 percent pay raise that grossed him $5.9 million after announcing the layoff of 25,000 workers in 1994. More than a few chief executives have publicly justified their outrageous paychecks by citing their track record of laying off employees and dismantling corporate operations.

Most of the million-a-year executives see little wrong with their lavish earnings. They hold a strong belief that they are entitled to their riches and that they have *earned* the money. James McKinney, a New York-based pay consultant, was likely voicing the feelings of many senior executives when he told a *Business Week* reporter: "Their greed isn't hurting anybody."

But is it? There are a number of management experts inside both academia and big business who suggest that these enormous payouts to executives may be doing irreparable damage. Respected University of Southern California management professor Warren Bennis notes, "There's a lot of rage out there. . . . Worried workers do not engage in the kind of creative problem-solving that contemporary business requires."

David Levine, professor at the Haas School of Business at Berkeley, conducted a study of eighty-nine organizations and found that those with the widest gaps in pay were also the lowest in quality. Levine found that these organizations weren't able to sustain a work environment of shared goals. Another study by Jeffrey Pfeffer of Stanford University found that greater discrepancies in pay go hand in hand with higher rates of employee turnover.

What is most disturbing about executive pay is that many organizations dealing with serious financial difficulties are willing to pay executives outrageous salaries even when there is little or no evidence that long-term gains are to be had from those executives' actions. On the one hand, these executives demand increasing compensation; on the other, they have absolutely no sympathy for the stagnant wages of workers or the increased workload dumped on employees after repeated layoffs, cost cutting, and restructurings.

Clearly, today's executive pay is an outgrowth of corporate narcissism. The strong feelings of grandiosity and entitlement among executives are symptomatic of the narcissist's obsession with personal gain and inability to empathize. A narcissist could never accomplish this on his own; only when the majority of corporate decision makers have colluded with him can he simultaneously acquire the power to reward himself and neglect those beneath him.

The Golden Ax

It is almost impossible to talk about executive compensation without a discussion of corporate layoffs. (For an in-depth discussion of this topic, see my book *Corporate Executions,* AMACOM, 1995.) The two trends have enjoyed parallel growth trends over the past fifteen years. While executive pay was creeping upwards in the early 1980s, so were the number of employees laid off each year.

The casualty estimates vary widely, ranging from the conservative figure of 3.1 million publicly announced layoffs since 1989 to the much-debated *New York Times* tally of 21.2 million in the same time period. The Bureau of Labor Statistics forecasts that one out of every twenty working Americans will get laid off this year. In 1995 alone, 440,000 employees were laid off, up 39 percent from 1990.

Downsizing, like executive pay, is driven by narcissistic self-interest. Wall Street believes downsizing equals lower wages and bigger profits, and rewards executives who announce big layoffs by driving up their company's stock price. Since these same executives own big chunks of stock, their net worth spirals up, just as their unlucky workers are wondering how they're going to make the mortgage payment. The narcissistic executive can then bask in the approval of Wall Street and haul in huge rewards in return for laying off employees.

As is characteristic in the narcissistic organization, the truth about a layoff is often in short supply. Ironically, many corporations announce that they are laying off employees to *improve* customer service, despite much evidence that shows layoffs usually diminish productivity, quality, and customer service. The truth is, most corporate layoffs are about lowering the company's labor costs (i.e., getting the same work done for less money). If the company were up front about this, there would be far more resistance from the retained employees. Instead, these companies choose to hide behind the complex rhetoric of reengineering and restructuring. Although it is true that a minority of corporate restructurings legitimately lead to layoffs, the majority of announced "restructurings" are simply a quick slimming of the payroll.

The narcissistic organization has turned inward. All of its resources are spent in satisfying the organization's endless desire for success as defined by its leaders. When a harsher reality contradicts its own grandiose fantasies, the organization chooses to retreat into the protection of those idealized fantasies. Replete with narcissistic leaders and a dependent management team, this organization blunders forward, adamantly resisting change and preserving the delicate balance of power orchestrated by its leaders.

FOUR

Where Winning Is All That Matters

Of Winners and Losers

I've always been a bit suspicious of the term "win-win." While the sentiment behind the concept is admirable, the definition of "win-win" is somewhat counterintuitive and self-canceling. After all, the word *win* would have no meaning without the word *lose*. So when one says that two parties have both won and neither lost (a "win-win" situation), the construct of winning loses all meaning. To *win* one must have two elements: a winner *and* a loser. The word "win" is forever doomed to describe a certain aspect of one-upmanship.

The concept of winning (and, consequently, losing) is very close to the narcissist's heart. The narcissist thrives on being the winner and derives ego strength by favorably comparing himself to the loser. If everyone were successful (as in "win-win"), the narcissist would have nothing from which he could derive his sense of superiority. To flourish, the narcissist must have losers on hand. If they don't exist, he creates them.

The narcissist isn't interested in the collective good (i.e., "win-win"), only in his personal triumphs. A situation that lacks competitiveness and where all are working for collective success is of no value to him. He gains nothing if there is no chance for him to stand out against a background of less-than-ideal colleagues.

Consequently, the narcissist must create in the organization a culture of ultra competitiveness. He forges a work environment where there are clear winners and losers, the winner takes all, and winning is to be had at any cost. Sometimes the cost of that "success" can be very great indeed.

STEVE JOBS AND THE LISA FIASCO

Most of the graduate students I have known, including myself, have rewritten their dissertations, cover to cover, a minimum of three, maybe four times. A document the size of a book, the dissertation is intended to further the field of study beyond its current state and must be approved by a committee of graduate professors who, more often than not, have diametrically opposed points of view. Trying to be true to one's own naïve ambitions and simultaneously win the approval of each committee member is a task that has destroyed many forests for the requisite paper.

I was in the middle of writing my dissertation when I encountered the "Lisa." I had typed and retyped so many pages, I was desperate for something that would make the task easier. My father, one of the earliest of the personal computer buffs, first introduced me to Lisa. One look and I was in love. Lisa, an Apple computer, was the most fascinating, easy-to-use computer I had ever seen. Just a click of a button and she could rearrange paragraphs of text or insert words into a sentence. She could do footnotes, tables of contents, indexes, and bibliographies with a few simple commands. Simple things, like switching from single-spaced to double-spaced text, could be done in a second, something that previously had required retyping the entire manuscript. Ecstatic, I must have sat for over an hour peering at the green phosphorous monitor and watching the salesperson caress the mouse as images danced across Lisa's screen.

Looking back, I realize how fortunate I was that Lisa

was out of the range of my pocketbook. The model was discontinued after six months and very few of them were made. Precious little software was written for this computer, which wasn't compatible with any other personal computer, Apple or otherwise. Although the press gushed over Lisa's user-friendly, icon-driven display and praised her ability to do complex tasks, her rise and fall occurred with unparalleled speed. Although very few knew it at the time, the world had witnessed in the Lisa the fallout of a corporate narcissistic struggle.

Computer Whiz-Kid

Steve Jobs is a creative talent and one-time whiz kid of the computer industry. Much to his credit, he cultivated Apple computers from a small mail order company in a garage to the internationally known entity it is today. The Lisa computer, named after his daughter, was his prized project. But when he became embroiled in a heated political battle at Apple, Steve also became a major force in her demise.

The Steve Jobs who founded Apple was as driven as he was talented. In the early days at Apple, he would work days on end without going home. Putting a dent in the universe, as he was fond of saying, was his primary objective. His obsession with work and neglect of his private life are legendary.

Not only did Steve approach his work with an almost monastic focus of mind and energy; he expected the same of his staff, too. He demanded long hours, high productivity, and endless patience with his sometimes scattered ideas. Only those who could keep pace with his manic energy lasted for any length of time.

For the most part, he demanded and got every ounce of commitment his staff could muster. His hypnotic charisma and the seductiveness of his dream hooked deep inside them and they, too, became obsessed with doing something meaningful and great, something that would quite literally change the course of history. Bill Atkinson, considered by many to be the most gifted programmer at Apple during the early days, said: "He can con you into believing his dream." *Time* magazine, in a 1983 feature article, described Steve as having "a smooth sales pitch and a blind faith that would have been the envy of the early Christian martyrs."[1]

By all accounts, it was Steve's drive and vision that brought Apple to the national spotlight. He was the force behind the creation and marketing of the Apple II, the computer that built the company from point zero to past the one billion mark. That feat forced Steve to use every resource at his disposal to make it happen, including, sometimes, guerrilla tactics that became well-known inside and outside Apple. It was no wonder that by the time the Apple II went to market, everyone at Apple was singing his praises from afar and no one wanted to work with him.

The Birth of Lisa

It was only natural that Steve would involve himself in the Lisa project, Apple's encore to the success of the Apple II. Over a period of six months, Steve, now Apple's president, meddled in the design of the computer, butting heads with the seasoned engineering manager, Ken Rothmueller, whom he had only recently hired from Hewlett Packard. Steve was determined to make this computer *his* computer, like no other before. Steve was haunted by the fact that while he had been the one who promoted the Apple II, it was his partner, Steve Wozniak, who had actually designed it. But not this time. Lisa was going to be his baby and he was determined to make it happen.

The only obstacle to Steve's eminence was the unfortunate fact that he had been forced to trade off company stock in exchange for capital to start Apple. In his early twenties at the time, he acquired financial backing from institutions that were run by men twice his age. Sensing an impetus and overzealous kid-turned-manager, they used the better part of wisdom and backed his company only after stipulating that more experienced partners be part of the day-to-day operations. While Steve remained the largest shareholder, the collective portions of the other investors outweighed his own shares. Steve was determined to prove to the other shareholders that he was entirely capable of bringing a product to market. Lisa was his perfect opportunity.

A brash, say-what-you-think and let-the-chips-fall-as-they-may style was Steve's mode of operation. He managed by edict, often making hundreds of on-the-spot decisions in a day that would have dramatic impact on the people and business of Apple Computers. Once, at the last minute, he changed an entire marketing campaign after reading a story he liked in *Scientific American* on, of all things, bicycle locomotion.[2]

Steve enforced his will with off-the-wall attacks that could come at any time. As Jeff Raskin, a former Apple publications manager, described him, "He's less sensitive to people's feelings. He runs over them, snowballs them. He would have made an excellent King of France."[3] Another Apple employee, who had worked closely with Steve, described him as a "doberman" who would "chew off the head" of anyone who stood in his way.[4]

With all of his engines running, Steve took the Lisa project by storm. The Lisa project manager, Ken Rothmueller, had already designed a bit-mapped, green phosphor monitor machine with a built-in keyboard. The machine was built around a new microprocessor from Motorola that was capable of much greater speed and complexity than the microprocessor in the Apple II. The look and feel of the machine were conservative, solid, and not particularly flashy. Ken had designed a Lisa model that was the complete antithesis of what Steve was all about, and he hated it. It was only a matter of time before Steve strong-armed Ken out of the picture and took over the Lisa project.

For Steve, the Lisa had to be something new; something sexy and easy to use. The only thing that Steve liked about Ken's machine was the use of the Motorola 68000, the newest and hottest thing in the business—so new it wasn't yet available. Steve discarded the rest of the design.

The Lisa, it had been decided, would be aimed at the somewhat nebulous business machine market, and Steve's idea of researching this market required little more than looking in the mirror. Without hesitation, Steve, the kid who had never worked in a real office environment or seen what the average office worker wanted in a personal computer, began single-handedly to decide the design of the machine that was to meet the computing needs of the office market. "We just went crazy," says Trip Hawkins, one of the leading members of the Lisa team. "Lisa became a kind of kitchen sink where we were trying to do everything that could possibly be done with a computer . . . "[5]

An Exclusive Club

Promoted and fueled by Steve, the Lisa project team became something of an elitist club within Apple that garnered the resentment of the other divisions. To begin with, employees had to have a bright orange badge just to be admitted into the building that housed the Lisa team. Further, Steve hired many well-trained, professional programmers to work on the project, not the typical young, do-it-by-your-instincts hackers that had traditionally populated Apple. Apple had always hired passionate amateurs who never outlined a program before writing, never wasted time on theoretical models, and thought that, for the most part, program comments were "for sissies."

Tensions at Apple began to rise and morale plummeted as Steve spoke disparagingly of the Apple II division to anyone who would listen. He said things like, it was "the dull and boring product division" at a time when the Apple II was extremely profitable and financing the rest of the company—including Steve's precious Lisa. He even told the press that Lisa would "leave the Apple II in the dust."

Reorganization

The rest of Apple senior management saw this storm brewing on the horizon and met unbeknownst to Steve to reorganize the company. The net result of the reorganization approved by the board of directors was that Steve was removed from any formal operating position. The directors gave the Lisa project to another manager, John Couch. Steve was shocked by the announcement and bitter at not having been consulted. He felt abandoned, and his ego was badly bruised. The Lisa project was more than just another computer; it was his vehicle to prove to the world that he could bring a product from design to market on his own.

As it turned out, the whole Lisa affair eventually cost Apple millions of dollars in both sunk cost and lost sales because of decisions that Steve had made early in development. His insistence that the Lisa have a graphical interface and a mouse like the one he had observed in Xerox's PARC laboratory drove the price up from the originally planned $2,000 to $10,000 and delayed the release of the computer by almost two years. While the graphical interface and mouse were among the most creative and ingenious improvements to the personal computer, history would show that the business market wasn't at all ready for a computer that appeared to operate like an advanced video game.

Not only was Lisa too expensive and elaborate for a market that had been well trained in the stilted interfaces of the mainframe; it cast a shadow of suspect over the little can-do company that had all the signs of a flash in the pan. Businesses demanded computing power and speed with large storage capabilities and assurances of service and support after the sale. Not seeing any of this fulfilled in the Lisa, the business market turned back to its comfortable partner, IBM. It was the failure of the Lisa that cinched an almost unanimous lockout of Apple from the colossal business machines market.

Lisa's Little Brother

Recovering only in appearance from the Lisa fiasco, Steve moved on in the following months to another project, the little brother to Lisa, called Macintosh. Wiser and more politically savvy, Steve had learned some hard lessons from Lisa and was determined not to make the same mistakes with the Macintosh.

The story of Steve's involvement with the Macintosh has

all the trappings of the guts and greed prime-time soap operas that were traveling the television airwaves during the early 1980s. To begin with, Steve located his hand-picked Macintosh design team in a building several miles from the rest of the Apple divisions, and he alone decided layout and office assignments. There he created the ultimate post-teenage work environment for the young programmers. A stereo with six-feet-high speakers was installed in the offices, and a Japanese masseur was placed on call for anyone in the group who worked late—all paid for by the company. The Macintosh refrigerator was stocked with fresh juices and mineral waters at a cost of $100,000 a year. As a larger-than-life reminder of his expectations of excellence, Steve placed a $50,000 Bossendorfer grand piano in the lobby of the office. The parking lot at the Texaco towers, the nickname of the building where the team was located, was filled with expensive European cars like BMWs and Saabs that Steve had arranged for the company to lease on behalf of the team. Whenever anyone from the Macintosh team flew on company business they flew first class, even when their fellow Apple employees who might be traveling with them were flying coach.

Without a doubt, the Macintosh team had Steve's undiluted attention. He would do anything to protect it from any outside interference. "All we had to do was complain about someone," a Macintosh team member said once, "and it was like unleashing a Doberman. He would chew the guy's head off so fast that our heads would spin." To protect the Macintosh from internal competition, he refused to allow the company to advertise the Apple II as a business computer, which was the market for which the Macintosh was being built. He used his status as a founder of the company to marshal all the funds and services he needed from other company managers. The Macintosh was his territory, and he did everything within his power to make it successful.

Steve wasn't an engineer, but that never stopped him from intervening in any technical meetings he walked in on. As far as Steve was concerned, any decision that affected *his* computer was fair game. He had his own definite ideas about its design. For one thing, he refused to allow the Macintosh to have a fan. Fans, he said, were required to correct inelegant design (despite the fact that hard disks required a fan). Further, to protect the elegance of what he created, he refused to allow for slots. To his way of thinking the Macintosh was to be a closed box; slots would allow people to add all sorts of devices that might corrupt his design. But perhaps the most unusual of all his design decisions was when he deliberately decided not to provide the Macintosh with a letter-quality printer. Even though hard disks, slots for hardware customization, and letter-quality print were all absolute musts of the business market, none were available with the original Macintosh. As the machine unfolded, two things became clear: Steve was listening to no one but himself, and when he made up his mind, nobody could change it.

When the time came to roll out the Lisa, Macintosh was six months away from introduction. Steve made the trip to New York for the introduction and filled a $575 dollar a night suite at the Hotel Carlyle with Lisas and a team of Apple managers who had worked on the project to unveil the machine before the press. It was Apple's first attempt at an orchestrated product introduction, and it was Steve's chance to shine.

Never was it clearer what the Lisa and Macintosh were all about. While introducing the revolutionary new Lisa before the press, Steve began describing not the Lisa, the project from which he had been forcibly and against his will removed, but his ego child, Macintosh. *Business Week* quoted Steve as saying "when it comes out, Mac is going to be the most incredible computer in the world—another Apple II."[6] He proudly described its features as "like Lisa" but at one quarter of the $10,000 Lisa price tag. With one fell stroke, he turned the fascination and awe over Lisa into excited anticipation for the Macintosh, which was scheduled to be released in six months. It's not surprising that buyers eagerly waited to see what was coming before investing in the Lisa, a reaction that killed the computer before it was ever really launched. The final kiss of death for Lisa was the surprising announcement that the Macintosh and Lisa would not be compatible, which meant if an office bought a Lisa, nothing would transfer to a Macintosh purchased in the future.

The Lisa project had been slain by Steve's narcissistic style. His intense need to win the race as he defined it in his own mind destroyed the Lisa and almost brought down the entire company. To Steve, Lisa and MacIntosh weren't about Apple computers or the customers who might want to purchase them; they were testimonies to *Steve's* abilities. When it became necessary for him to destroy Lisa to restore his image, he did so in the blink of an eye.

By all accounts, Steve was never really into computers. "Steve didn't do one circuit, design or piece of code. He's not really been into computers and to this day he has never gone through a computer manual," one prominent Apple engineer noted. Another Apple manager commented about "the technical ignorance he's not willing to admit." The personal computer happened to be an ingenious idea that he came across while growing up in the technologically affluent Silicon Valley. It was an ingenious device that made the rest of the world notice its features—and its creator.

Without hesitation and at every turn, Steve assumed the role of the whiz-kid creator. One not-so-subtle instance occurred when Steve changed the advertising copy of a nationwide Apple campaign at the last minute from "I" to "we" in the slogan: "When *I* created the Personal Computer, *I* created a New Generation of Entrepreneurs." Several years later, looking back on his accomplishments, he again preempted the credit for Apple successes: "*I* did it in the garage when Apple started, and *I* did it in the metaphorical garage when Mac started."

To Steve's credit, when the Macintosh was finally introduced, it was by all accounts the most innovative, user-friendly personal computer the world had ever seen. It was hailed by the press and landed Steve on the cover of *Time* and *Life* magazines. Anyone who had suffered through the early morning hours in a computer room keypunching programs on cards or struggled with strings of tedious, archaic commands couldn't believe that so much power could be put in such a small box and made so easy—even fun—to use. It used hard-core, commonplace analogies that everyone could understand, like a desktop, file folders, and a tool box, and placed them all neatly on the screen, eliminating the need to remember operating system commands. The design was so revolutionary that the ideas behind the user-friendly Macintosh interface would go on to influence the design of computer software for at least the next decade.

THE PRICE OF TYRANNICAL NARCISSISM

To criticize the young, ambitious Jobs, the kid who was separated from high school and Chairman of the Board by only a few years, has the distinct tinge of sour grapes. After all, despite his inexperience, he took a company from a suburban garage to multi-billion dollar sales in a miraculously short time. The dream of every new MBA is undoubtedly to be so successful in a lifetime career, much less before the age of twenty-five. Sure, he made some mistakes and might be difficult to work with, but doesn't that high-powered drive and creativity always bear the price of such eccentricities? Anyone who has tried to create the future by leading a group of people to make something that goes above and beyond what exists today would surely agree that his tyrannical management style is but a small price to pay given the enormous task he undertook. Steve's achievements have reached the level of folklore for those in the high tech industry, and as folklore heroes do, he lived the story that so many have only dreamed.

But the story of Steve Jobs is a story of narcissism. Jagged and raw narcissism in all of its strength and glory—narcissism that wasn't trained in subtlety and finesse by experience and age. Consider a few of the facts: First, neither the Lisa nor the Macintosh was designed according to the business objective the company had committed them to. The critical design features of both were driven by Steve's need to be creative and different from the mainstream. Further, while Steve was working with the Macintosh group, he intentionally acted in ways that were damaging to both the Apple II and Lisa, even though as a major stockholder he stood to benefit greatly from their successes. It was more important that the Macintosh, the project he had invested himself in, be seen as superior. Finally, Steve sought out and accepted public recognition as the creator of Apple's successes when he was only one of several very talented people who made the company. Steve never designed a circuit or program for any of the Apple computers. Using Apple Computers as a platform and computers as the straight man, Steve bathed his ego in the warmth of public applause. It was a place that he created not to make computers, but to make computers that would bear his unmistakable signature.[7]

Like Steve, the narcissist is obsessed with winning the race as he or she defines it. Steve wasn't trying to win the race to sell the most business machines—the final MacIntosh was clearly not a business computer. He was in a breakneck race to produce the sexiest, most clever machine that would leave the hulking Lisa in the dust. He sacrificed everything to win.

Success to the narcissist is a personal victory and the bottom line is personal gain. Collective good and corporate enhancement are only a pretext to his real goals. In the case of Steve Jobs, his own need to be seen as a heroic computer designer and manager led him to eclipse the best interest of Apple Computers.

KEEPING SCORE

The narcissistic obsession with winning manifests itself not only in costly internal conflicts, as with the Lisa and MacIntosh computers, but also in a romance with quantifiable indices of performance. Simply put, you can't win a race if someone isn't keeping score.

Corporate scorecards measure what is measurable, and what isn't is often discarded by the narcissist. To say one increased profits by 10 percent or decreased customer returns by 4 percent creates the illusion of a solid victory. If, on the other hand, a manager claims he increased employee motivation or improved the company's relationship with a critical supplier, he will have a difficult time marketing these victories among senior management. Even if these aspects of the business are more important than other, quantifiable areas, they appear "soft" and subjective. Non-quantifiable victories don't make good sound bites and consequently aren't very useful in the narcissist's personal PR campaign.

The narcissistic organization becomes obsessed with quantifiable indices of performance: "The numbers tell it all." "Above all, you have to make your numbers." "I don't care *how* he does it, all I know is that he makes his numbers."

In the 1970s corporate history took a dramatic change in course. For the first time ever, two separate academic disciplines converged and began producing highly educated graduates ready for careers as professional managers. These two academic programs, one in management and the other in behavioral science, have left an unmistakable imprint on today's corporation. These two ideologies share one powerful and unquestioned assumption: All accurate business decisions must be based on quantifiable data. Of most importance to the narcissistic manager is that the majority of management compensation is based on these "hard" criteria.

LYING NUMBERS

But the numbers can be made to lie, and no one knows this better than the narcissist. For instance, by selling assets of the business, profits can be made to jump and give the appearance of a company that is healthy and productive. Costs can be driven down at the expense of the future growth of the company. Quality statistics can be made to improve by increasing the reliability of materials even when the new materials are still inadequate to meet customer needs.

In a wonderfully entertaining little book, *How to Lie with Statistics*,[8] Darrell Huff chronicles many of the more common techniques used to "cook the books." One of the many examples Huff describes regards the numbers measuring business performance. In the 1950s the grocery store chain A & P reported that it had earned 1.1 percent on sales. Many considered this figure distressingly low and, indeed, letters published in *Harper's* magazine suggested that perhaps A & P would be better off getting out of the grocery business and investing its capital in the bank.

Huff goes on to explain that earnings on total sales is not the same as annual return on investment. A & P was actually doing quite nicely with return on investment. Huff explains it this way: If a retailer purchases one product every morning for ninety-nine cents and sells it that afternoon for a dollar, the retailer has earned only one percent on total sales, but 365 percent on invested capital for the year.

Depending on the choice of number and method of measurement, numbers can be easily manipulated. The narcissist focuses on how he can influence the numbers in his direction. Like the college student who prefers to read the *Cliff Notes* and memorize answers from bootlegged exams, he tries to circumvent the process of good management by influencing the metrics of outcome, not the outcome itself. Should his performance ever be called into question, he can point to his quantified report card as evidence of his stellar performance.

Consequently, the narcissistic manager has found a patron in the corporate reengineering movement. Sharpen the ax and crack the whip, because costs and productivity measure quite nicely. And in the immediate returns, this may work. But over the long haul, the hidden, future costs—something else that isn't easily measured—come back to haunt the balance sheet. This is the point where the short-term thinking of today's narcissism creates tomorrow's time bomb—an explosion set just far enough into the future to obliterate the original cause.

CUTTING BOTH COSTS AND SAFETY

A tragic example of a company that focused on the quantitative aspects of profit and business growth but ignored some of the less quantifiable aspects of safety happened in May 1996 when a ValuJet DC–9 crashed into the Florida Everglades, killing all 110 persons aboard. In the days and weeks following that much-publicized disaster, it became painfully apparent that the crash was not an unfortunate mishap but one incident in a string of many safety lapses.

It seems that during its three years of operation ValuJet had earned the reputation of having one of the highest accident rates and safety violations of any commercial carrier.[9] The Federal Aviation Administration (FAA) had conducted two special investigations of the airline before the 1996 crash and one afterwards. Each investigation uncovered numerous safety problems violations that appeared to be related to ValuJet's low-cost operation. In one of the the most striking incidents, a nineteen-year-old DC–9 loaded with passengers taking off from Boston was forced to make an unscheduled return after the landing gear would not retract properly. The plane was then flown empty to Dulles International for service, but en route the landing gear worked fine, so the plane was immediately put back in passenger service without any repairs. Other safety violations included using mechanics who were unqualified and inexperienced, ignoring serious fire hazards, and flying planes known to have nonfunctioning weather radar. The FAA's list of egregious violations was long and varied.[10]

Aside from safety, ValuJet's short history was spectacular. From its start in 1993 it had grown from 2 airplanes and 8 routes to 51 planes and 3 hubs in 1996. Within two months after the first flight, ValuJet was continuously profitable, something virtually unheard of in the tumultuous airline industry. Wall Street loved the little airline and after an initial stock offering in June 1994, the stock rose sharply, with a two-for-one stock split in April 1995 and a second split the following November.[11]

The airline's secret to financial success was its focus on lowering costs. It pioneered the ticketless booking system now used by many airlines. It purchased a fleet of similar planes to reduce training and maintenance costs. It contracted out most of its mechanical service. It eliminated in-flight meals. It paid personnel, including pilots and flight attendants, the lowest salaries in the industry. It even required pilots to pay for some of their own training costs.[12]

ValuJet's founders, four airline veterans, decided to run their company with the lowest cost in the industry. Their extreme cost-conscious management failed to calculate the less quantifiable cost of reduced safety. Ultimately, ValuJet's negligence cost the airline four months of business after the FAA temporarily shut down the entire operation for compliance violations. The cost of that mistake totaled in the millions of dollars.

Miami Herald business editor Beatrice Garcia questioned whether the mislabeled oxygen containers would have been loaded onto the plane if the cargo handlers had been ValuJet employees. Perhaps they would have been more attentive had it been their own company's future they risked? No one can say for certain. Employee loyalty and motivation are difficult if not impossible to measure. One can only wonder if it would have made a difference at ValuJet.

DEPARTING FROM REALITY

Sometimes the need to win can push the narcissistic organization to deny reality. This is especially true when a previous rush of success starts to trickle out; the narcissistic organization may pretend that disaster isn't lurking. In some cases, like Bausch & Lomb, they may even try to rewrite the scene to fit a grander image.

MAKE THE NUMBERS

Bausch & Lomb, America's venerable optical company, enjoyed double-digit growth in both sales and earnings throughout the 1980s. In 1980 Dan Gill, a rising star from Abott Laboratories, was made president of the stodgy manufacturer of optical equipment, eyeglass lenses, and contact lenses. Young and ambitious, Gill dove into B&L's business with the savvy of a financial analyst and a salesman's charm. Without wasting time, Gill refocused B&L's business by selling several inefficient optical businesses, growing profitable divisions, and pushing the company abroad.

Determined to improve B&L's financial, Gill created a hard-driving, demanding culture where, according to several former executives, the numbers were all-important. Gill began his career as an auditor and as CEO he would regularly examine each division's monthly financial report. One executive remembers, "He had a tremendous ability to stay on top of financial details."

Gill's goal was double-digit annual growth, and no division was exempt. Former B&L President Thomas McDermott recalls, "Once you signed up for your target number, you were expected to reach it." At one teleconference, the head of European operations was grilled for not making his numbers, despite the fact that the shortfall was in the currency fluctuations. By local currency standards he was right on target.

To push his philosophy through the organization, Gill restructured B&L's compensation system to reward growth in revenue. Former executives report that division heads were given hefty bonuses for meeting or exceeding targets, while falling short by as little as 10 percent could eliminate the bonus altogether. Most notably, little to no weight was given to asset management and customer service. According to one B&L manager, "You could miss your asset objectives by a mile and still get a big payday."

One famous Gill line was: "Make the numbers, but don't do anything stupid." Ironically, as one marketing executive noted, the only stupid thing you could do was not make the numbers.

The message from the top pushed some executives to cut corners. Managers, eager to maximize their bonus, started using tactics that were costly to the company. Bonus-

maximizing practices abounded, such as extending unusu-
ally long credit terms to customers in exchange for big orders
and shipping inventory to customers but not requiring payment until the customer sold the inventory. When the end
of the fiscal quarter approached, account managers would
often panic and start offering money off, or extra thirty to
sixty days payment terms. While these moves boosted sales
volume, they dramatically hurt margins. Customers quickly
discovered the end-of-quarter scramble and started withholding orders until the good deals were offered.

The lumping of orders into the frantic days at the end
of the quarter made B&L's distribution system bog down to
a standstill. Its Ray-Ban distribution center in San Antonio,
Texas, was forced to stay open twenty-four hours a day for
the last few days of every quarter. To meet the demand, up
to thirty-five temporary workers were hired and full-time
staff hauled in huge overtime checks. "We'd ship 70 percent
of the quarter's goods in the last three days," says a former
operations manager.

Gill's hard-driving efforts paid off. Between 1980 and
1991 sales increased from $441 million to $1.5 billion and
the stock had risen a remarkable fivefold.

With the success, Gill indulged in the extravagances of
the rich and famous. B&L bought a three-plane fleet and
built an elegant private terminal at the Rochester, New York,
airport. He began using the company planes for personal
trips to his home in Florida and a private fishing club in Can-
ada. By 1991, Gill's total compensation had reached $6.5
million, an eighteenfold gain from his first year as CEO. To
top it all off, Gill commissioned a brand new $70 million
headquarters to house his office.

By the early 1990s, B&L's financial picture began to
darken. Growth was slowing in the United States and Eu-
rope. Several big acquisitions were losing money. Ray-Bans
had fallen out of style. And the worst of all, Johnson & Johnson had caught B&L completely off-guard with introduction
of disposable contact lenses, further eroding B&L's share of
that market.

The pressure to make aggressive sales targets didn't let

up. *Business Week* reported that one Northeast district ordered reps to simply ship packages worth $1,600 to $2,400 containing a new multifocal lens to every account, even if they hadn't ordered it. Several hundred doctors were shipped lenses they didn't order, and the shipments were then booked as sales.

But the worst happened in December 1993, when B&L called a meeting of about thirty of its distributors. In that meeting they were told to take huge shipments of older contact lenses—up to two years' worth—and threatened to sever their distributorship ties if they refused. All but two agreed, and B&L booked an extra $23 million in revenue during the final days of 1993. Not surprisingly, six months into 1994, most of the lenses were returned and the distributors en masse refused to pay for them. The fiasco eventually led to an SEC investigation into the questionable accounting practices.

Shortly afterwards in 1994, auditors discovered an unaccounted for warehouse full of Ray-Ban sunglasses in Hong Kong. After some investigation, it was discovered that the sales had been faked and the sunglasses dumped in a warehouse—all in an effort to meet the Asia-Pacific division's sales targets. Prior to this scandal, the head of the Asia-Pacific division, Y. H. Chan, had become something of a hero around the Rochester corporate headquarters. Gill was happy with Chan's sales and never once questioned his methods. According to some executives, as long as he met his numbers, Gill was happy.

In typical narcissistic fashion, Gill reserved little blame for himself. "It's generally accepted that day-to-day operations of a company are overseen by the chief operating officer," says. "I don't mean to pass the buck, but . . . as chairman I'd have only a general understanding of what happened." As for any breaches of ethics, Gill says, "We think we are the most honorable beings on the face of the earth."

One former executive remembers a videotape presentation featuring Gill that was produced after the SEC investigation in 1994. In the video, Gill blamed the problems on the divisional presidents and proclaimed the divisions needed closer monitoring. "It was like slapping the hands of children," says this executive, "when they were really acting on Daddy's orders."

Dan Gill was ousted as head of B&L in January of 1996. Shortly thereafter, interim CEO William Waltrip restated the company's 1993 and 1994 earnings. The new figures reflect approximately $17 million difference in income for each year. As of this writing, the SEC investigation into questionable accounting practices at B&L continues.

WINNING IS EVERYTHING

The case of B&L illustrates what happens in the narcissistic organization when the compulsion to win overshadows all other concerns. The growth in revenue and earnings became an addiction that drove the company into highly questionable practices. When the markets wouldn't bear the growth, the company refused to accept this reality and began creating a fantasy that supported the image Dan Gill demanded of the company.

What this case clearly shows is the power of a narcissistic leader over the organization. Dan Gill never had to engage in questionable or illegal activities. Furthermore, he may have never directly asked anyone else to engage in such practices. He simply established an organizational system where the primary goal was to support the image of B&L that he wanted to see. Management, inventory, and information systems were all designed to fulfill the targets he set. His staff, eager to comply and achieve company-rewarded success, did all the work.[13]

FIVE

Profit and the Dark Side

The narcissistic obsession with winning can be more like a personal quest than a corporate endeavor. Although unbridled ambitions for success are nothing new, in the narcissistic organization, they flourish. Blinded by incessant cravings, the line between what is right and wrong, ethical and not, can become less definite for the corporate narcissist. Sometimes it disappears altogether.

BLACK MARKET CHIPS

Eric and I had taken a long lunch away from the office that particular day. It was one of those lunches that replaced a meeting we couldn't schedule during regular hours, so we had eaten and worked for a good two hours before we returned to the office. As we pulled into a parking stall next to the back door of the building, I noticed someone was thrashing about in the hunter green BMW next to us. As we both turned to get a better look, it was clear that someone was pulling a stereo or something with a lot of wires out of the console of the car. I looked and then really looked, not be-

lieving my eyes—that someone was George . . . Mr. Black
. . . President and CEO George Black! He slammed the car
door and quickly walked into the building with a rainbow of
wires trailing behind him.

This was high corporate drama and we were fast behind
to find out what we could. As George passed the back lobby
receptionist, he dropped what we later discovered was a
car phone into the waste basket and without missing one
determined step disappeared into the executive wing. Then
there were the police . . . and Ed Snyder in handcuffs . . .
and the hysterical secretary . . . and for weeks afterwards the
office was swarmed with news reporters.

What we discovered in the following hours and days
was that George had uncovered Ed's black market side business of selling the company's computer chips. Ed had been
George's "golden boy" and close friend. It was well known
that Ed and George played tennis every Sunday at George's
house—an event that was known by everyone in the company as the "Sunday strategy meeting." When George discovered that he had been undercut by someone he had
trusted as much as he had Ed, he acted out his anger in the
most visible and violent way he could quickly imagine: He
ripped out the company-issued car phone from Ed's car. It
was a ridiculous, perhaps even childish move, but it had all
the violent symbolism of a corporate castration.

Shortly after the fiasco, I heard that despite Ed's
$200,000 plus salary he was on the verge of bankruptcy. A
7,000-square-foot home on one of the most prestigious golf
courses in the country, top-of-the-line import cars, and a
condo in Las Vegas were but a few of the expensive trinkets
that were breaking his bank account. Even though in time
he would have had the title of CEO and the paycheck that
goes with it, he couldn't wait. Grandeur was singing, and he
was mesmerized by the melody.

Although every day a few brazen employees cross the line
of ethics to grab an extra share of profit, most narcissistic lead-

ers are too savvy for such an overt move. They can't afford the risk involved in direct illegal activities or the risk of commanding their subordinates to do the same. Instead, they set performance objectives impossibly high. These leaders then look the other way as employees are forced either to compromise their ethics or fail.

This is the ideal racket for a narcissist. Should the compromised employee get caught, the narcissist can scapegoat him and deflect the guilt. He benefits from the employee's questionable activity and, at the same time, protects himself from identification with the wrongdoing. In this way, a few narcissistic leaders can push an entire organization to cross moral, ethical, and even legal limits.

SAMURAI MANAGEMENT

Take, for example, the number one software database company: Oracle Systems Corp. In 1981, when IBM decided to allow all of its products to support a database query language called "SQL," Larry Ellison saw his opportunity. He left IBM and formed Oracle Systems Corp. Oracle's first product was complete rewrite of SQL allowing it to run on any computer. As IBM pumped out its new PCs, Oracle boomed.

Ellison intentionally patterned his management style after medieval samurai warriors. He stormed the database market by attacking his competitor's products and touting the benefits of Oracle. From 1981 to 1988 the company doubled in size each year, reaching $282 million in revenue.

By all accounts, Ellison's damn-the-torpedoes style of management flourished with the success. He let no one stand in his way. Symbolic of his utter disregard for limits, employees relish the story of how Ellison knowingly sped his sports car through the same speed trap three days in a row, pulling into Oracle's parking lot with police sirens blaring behind him.

But trouble was on the horizon: Its name was competition. In 1990, Oracle began making promises it could not keep (described by *Success* magazine as "blatant lies"). Driven by its warlord chief executive, Oracle began losing ground. Unwilling to accept a slowdown, Ellison—the company's major shareholder—launched version 6.0 of the company's trademark software long before all of the errors had been worked out. The software was so bug infested, clients couldn't run it. The company falsely claimed in huge trade magazine ads that the software was compatible with IBM's DB 2 database. Some industry insiders began joking that the only research and development at Oracle was done on an overhead projector. According to former employees, it was no joke.

The sales force began to use the same tactics. They would make outrageous promises to close a deal. Often they would give incredible credit contracts and would book sales long before a contract was signed.

Customers were furious at having bought a product whose capabilities were oversold. One customer, the high tech consulting firm Dataquest, was among those burned by Oracle. Dataquest analyst Paul Cubbage said, "They listen a lot. It's almost a form of grief counseling."

One particular software package performed so poorly that Cubbage asked Oracle if the product was actually ready for the market. The company admitted that it wasn't. "They promised the world and delivered somewhat less."

One former Oracle salesperson told the *San Jose Mercury News* that the company was so determined to meet its sales targets that it only cared about those customers ready to make a purchase during the current quarter. "It created a very short-term mentality," he said.[1]

In September 1990, it came crashing down. The company was finally forced to post a $28.7 million loss, sending its shares spiraling downward from $28 to $5.37 a share. The company lost 80 percent of its $3.7 billion market capitalization, and the Securities and Exchange Commission launched an investigation into Oracle's fraudulent accounting practices.[2]

What did Ellison do? He blamed the lapses in ethics on

several chief lieutenants and went on a firing spree. Hundreds of executives were canned, and even more quit in fear. Ellison put on quite a show hoping to regain the trust of Wall Street.

Whether Ellison was personally involved in the fraudulent practices, as several former executives claim, isn't the issue. The point is, Ellison knowingly created a corporate culture that drove employees beyond the boundaries of ethical limits. By molding the organization's financial goals, he profited handsomely without being accused of personal wrongdoing. With a personal fortune of over $3 billion, he is regularly listed among Silicon Valley's wealthiest CEOs.[3]

BEST OF INTENTIONS

Very often, the employees of the narcissistic organization have the best intentions. They are ethical, decent people who are willing to work hard for success. They would never intentionally engage in activities that are adverse to society. Yet it is these very same employees who carry out the mission of the narcissistic leader.

By following the corporate objectives without questioning the broader impact of those actions, employees can unwittingly become accomplices in some very destructive activities. Each employee simply does his small part, which, when considered separately, may not be all that bad. When considered in the context of the cumulative organizational response, however, the combined impact of many employees engaged in borderline activities can be quite sinister. The organization becomes something of a shield that prevents any one individual from accepting responsibility for the organization's actions. In this way, a few narcissistic leaders can use the organization to accomplish otherwise unthinkable acts.

Another way narcissistic leaders can steer an organization across the line of ethics is to control the information employees receive on company operations. In today's world, where multinational corporate operations are common, it is virtually impossible for any one employee to be familiar with all the details of company maneuvers. Knowing this, the narcissistic leader allows employees to learn only the favorable aspects of the truth. By shielding employees from the unethical or illegal ramifications of their actions, well-meaning employees become participants in activities they would have never engaged in had they been completely knowledgeable.

WHITEWASHING THE TRUTH

Freeport-MacMoRan, a New Orleans, Louisiana-based company, exemplifies what happens when the twin obsessions for profit and image control an organization. Freeport has become extremely profitable through some environmentally disastrous businesses while promoting itself as a corporate protector of the environment. Using an internal and external public relations campaign combined with a "strategic" philanthropy program, Freeport has attempted to whitewash some highly questionable activities, including the use of a foreign military to relocate a village of indigenous peoples; the destruction of hundreds of acres of virgin rain forest; contamination the groundwater of a major metropolitan area—they are the number one corporate polluter in the U.S., according to the Environmental Protection Agency; and, close association with the murder of sixteen critics of their Indonesian operations.

The main source of Freeport's controversy is its copper and gold mine, located in the virgin rain forests of Irian Jaya, the western half of the island commonly known as New Guinea. A primitive and lush territory, Irian Jaya is poor in industrialization and very rich in natural resources and minerals.

Since 1962, when it was annexed from the Dutch, Irian Jaya has been a territory in the country of Indonesia. The native peoples of the territory, mostly of the Amunge tribe, live a very primitive existence, dependent upon jungle vegetation and the bounty of the rivers for their sustenance. Clothed with little more than loincloths, they live simply, enmeshed in an ancient culture that predates that of the Western world.

Among other things, the Amunge consider the volcanic mountains that tower above their densely treed valleys to be sacred. They have worshipped these mountains for centuries, never knowing or caring that they were filled with rich deposits of copper, gold, and other precious minerals. In the 1960s, a geologist employed by the company's precursor, Freeport Minerals, discovered these minerals in Irian Jaya.

Greed Moves In

Ironically, the minerals discovered in those mountains are also sacred to the fiscal systems of the rest of the world. In 1967, then-General Suharto took control of Indonesia by military coup and became President, an office he has continually held up to the present. More of a dictatorship than a democracy, Suharto has ruled Indonesia with a heavy hand under the rubric of consensus and the development of commerce. He is known to crush any opposition to his agenda with military force. His violent takeover of East Timor and subsequent mass executions—labeled a war of cultural differences—was condemned by the United Nations. At present, the U.N. has refused to acknowledge the acquisition of East Timor by Indonesia.

Suharto signed the original agreement with Freeport in 1967 giving the company 250,000 acres of the Amunge's ancestral lands and a three-year holiday from taxes. The Amunge, having no concept of land ownership, compensation, or mining, were paid ten cents an hour to build roads for Freeport. After that, they were transferred to resettlement camps along the coastal lowland, where many died of malaria.[4]

As the Amunge learned firsthand what had happened to their sacred mountain, resentment toward Freeport and the Indonesian military grew. Their rivers, Aghawagon, Otomona, and Ajkwa, became polluted with the 115,000 tons of dusty mine tailings dumped into the rivers by Freeport each year. By accounts other than those of consultants hired by Freeport, the tailings contain copper, which is toxic to most aquatic organisms and has created significant acid run-off. By all accounts, more than fifty square miles of rain forest have been destroyed by the operation.

The OPM began sporadic sabotage of the mine, which climaxed in 1977 when stolen Freeport explosives were used to blow up a copper slurry pipe and temporarily shut-down the operation. That incident was followed by the Indonesian Army's Operasi Tumpas (Operation Annihilation), a mass slaughter that killed anywhere from 900 to several thousand of the Amunge and sympathetic tribesmen.

President Suharto has continually employed the military to protect Freeport, his country's largest taxpayer. The Amunge are kept in check by the army, which Amnesty International describes in a 1995 report on Irian Jaya as engaging in "a continuing pattern" of "political imprisonment, torture, ill-treatment and extrajudicial execution." One tribesman, for example, was beheaded for participating in a flag raising ceremony.

A variety of reports from international organizations have documented other Freeport-related atrocities. In 1988, according the Rainforest Action Network, Freeport relocated 1,000 residents to coastal lowlands and the army moved in to burn down their old huts. The Australian Council for Overseas Aid reports the disappearance of thirty-seven O.P.M sympathizers since June of 1994. The same report details a Christmas Day 1995 incident where three tribesmen were killed when the army opened fire on an Amunge ceremony held near Freeport property to honor their ancestors. Thirteen others were arrested and tortured. In March of 1996, Indonesian troops killed at least six people and arrested eighty-nine others associated with a Freeport demonstration.[5]

Although Freeport has never been shown to be directly associated with the army's actions, there are a number of suspicious links. The most convincing comes from a report released by the Catholic Church of Jayapura, the Roman

Catholic diocese of the Irian Jaya territory. That report details numerous incidents of killings and tortures by the army since mid-1994 near Freeport property. According to the Church, most of the clashes occurred while people were protesting what they considered to be inadequate compensation by the company for mining their land.[6]

Another indicator that Freeport may be behind the military's actions comes from the fact that many of the locals confuse the military with Freeport employees. Members of the military are regularly transported in Freeport's buses and housed in the company compound. Further, Freeport's own security officers have been seen to work in coordination with the local military command. WALHI, an Indonesian-based organization that monitors Freeport, was told by an army general that Freeport helps to pay the salaries of the seventy military personnel who patrol the mine. By Freeport's own admission, the line between the army and the company has been at times blurred.

Poisoning the Land

The environmental problems of the mine are somewhat difficult to assess, since Freeport security limits access to the roads leading to the mine (the only roads in the area) and Freeport operates the only airport on the island. Nevertheless, in 1995 the Overseas Private Investment Corporation (OPIC) canceled Freeport's insurance policy on the mine, citing serious environmental concerns. OPIC, a quasi-U.S. governmental agency that insures American companies doing business abroad, terminated the policy specifically because of increased mine tailings, which are choking the rivers and flooding the rain forests.

The acid runoff from the mine has already killed one mountaintop lake, which Freeport has now filled in. According to the company, the lake never supported anything other than microscopic life before they decided to cover it over. Critics claim the brilliant turquoise lake was one of the few lakes previously untouched by man in the world, and biologists in particular consider it an enormous loss.[7]

The OPIC cancellation brought public attention to the problems of Freeport in Irian Jaya. Clearly, the cancellation created an image that was not of the company's liking. To counteract, Freeport stepped up its public relations efforts both inside and outside the company. The campaign painted a very different picture of the company's $50 billion Indonesian mine.

Damage Control

CEO "Jim Bob" Moffett led the charge to bolster Freeport's tarnished image. A video released with Moffett's voice-over declares that mining causes "absolutely no damage to the forests" and "no acid drainage problems." As for the indigenous tribes, they "are moving into the twenty-first century." Indignant with Freeport's critics, Moffett declared that Freeport was "thrusting a spear of economic development into the heartland of Irian Jaya."[8]

The company publicized the fact that it employed some of the native Amunge at the mine and had spent $14 million a year on social-welfare projects. The company constructed a modern town that included houses, schools, and clinics for the local people.

Omitted from Freeport's self-congratulatory response was the fact that the company had to build much of this for their transplanted employees, regardless of the needs of the local people. In addition, the company failed to mention that only 14 percent of the mine's employees were local and of those, most were making less than $1,000 a month. Further, the company seems to have forgotten that the $14 million a year spent on local projects is less than one percent of the company's total revenues—a small price to pay the Amunge for billions of dollars in gold.

Halfway around the world and inside the company headquarters in New Orleans, another public relations war was being waged. Freeport was determined to convince its own employees that all was well with the mine. A public relations firm owned by a local television anchor, Garland Robinette, produced videos about the mine and its problems. Two local environmental reporters were hired to produce "Focus Earth" infomercials to be shown on New Orleans local television and in schools. Full-page advertisements in national newspapers, including the *New York Times*, proclaimed the innocence of Freeport.

The reception of this public relations onslaught—what *The Wall Street Journal* called "shooting a howitzer at a mosquito"—was something less than positive, and internally, many of Freeport's own employees still weren't convinced. Bruce Marsh, senior manager of environmental and public affairs for Freeport's Indonesian affiliate, PT Freeport Indonesia, said the videos so oversimplified the problems that he would resign before showing them in Indonesia.

Emmy Hafild of the environmental group WALHI compared Freeport's campaign to a boomerang: The harder they throw it, the more criticism of Freeport it brings. Hafild and many other environmental experts criticized the environmental and social audits released by Freeport. These reports, which exonerated the company of any adverse environmental or human rights violations, were written by consultants who were paid by Freeport. They have refused to release their raw data for public analysis.[9]

All of this backlash infuriated Moffett and his senior managers. When local students from Loyola University protested in front of his mansion on stately St. Charles Avenue in New Orleans, he demanded that the University give back his $600,000 donation. That donation had been given several years earlier to found an environmental studies program at the university.[10]

Moffett was quick to call on other recipients of Freeport money, which included $50 million in local philanthropy, gifts to five Louisiana universities, and the sponsorship of a local PGA golf tournament. Not surprisingly, the New Orleans City Council, Chamber of Commerce, and several prominent academicians offered public support and praise of Freeport. (One council member said privately that the council was just "sucking up" to Freeport.[11]) The local newspaper, *The New Orleans Times-Picayune*, published a series of full-page articles on Freeport's activities in Irian Jaya. The

articles recanted the company's generous philanthropy program to local charities and relied heavily on information
from Freeport executives that, not surprisingly, cast the mine
in a positive light.

When three Texas professors, including one anthropol-
ogist who had studied Indonesian islands for years, continued to criticize Freeport, Senior Vice President Thomas Egan
fired off letters threatening to sue the professors if they persisted. Those threats eventually led to the resignation of the
Chancellor of the University of Texas System, William Cunningham, from a $40,000 a year job as a member of Free-
port board of directors.[12]

Image Obsessed

What is most interesting about the Freeport case is not
whether the company was guilty of extreme environmental
damage or human rights violations but the response of the
company to these charges. Freeport is obsessed with creating an image of itself as environmental leader, when, in fact,
it clearly is not.

According to 1993 figures from the U.S. Environmental
Protection Agency, Freeport pumped 193.6 million pounds
of toxic material into the air, water, and soil, nearly three
times as much as America's next largest polluter. Since the
1970s, Freeport has stacked radioactive phosphogypsum
near its home base in New Orleans, creating a phosphoric
acid and heavy metal leak into the local ground water. In
1984, Freeport petitioned for an exemption to the Clean
Water Act to off-load 25 billion pounds of toxic waste annually into the Mississippi River. Eventually, that petition was
denied by the Louisiana Department of Environmental
Quality.

Other anti-environmental activities of Freeport include
membership in the Clean Water Coalition and the National
Wetlands Coalition, both of which are lobbying groups for
the rollback of environmental legislation. In Austin, Texas,
Freeport hired ten lobbyists (five were paid $25,000–
$49,000) to convince the Texas legislature to relax Austin's

water quality ordinances and allow the company to dump sewage into a popular recreational river. To this end, Freeport was even successful in convincing a reporter from the *Austin-American Statesman* to write a series of fawning articles about the company. That reporter now works for Freeport.

Eventually, however, the company's hardball tactics in Austin turned public opinion against the company, and the initiative failed. Moffett proclaimed a modern-day curse on the city, publicly announcing that "no Fortune 500 company is coming to Austin after what we've been through."[13]

At the same time, Freeport continues to spend millions of dollars creating the image of a corporate environmental leader. Television ads show Freeport involved in preventing wetland erosion along Louisiana's marshy coastline, and full-page spreads in business magazines recount Freeport's gifts to universities for environmental studies and the Louisiana Nature Conservancy. The company founded its own environmental group called the Environmental Research Consortium of Louisiana, whose stated goal is "the preservation of our planet through the sharing of ideas and resources." Even the company slogan, "giving something back," is designed to imply that Freeport is doing something for the environment.

Freeport is a prime example of what happens when a company becomes obsessed with its image and is equally obsessed with increasing profit. The company has used a variety of tactics to hide private and sometimes remote environmental blunders behind a public image of an environmentally responsible corporation. Because the real issues are spread across several continents and oceans, the company has had moderate success in altering the picture of its actions as viewed by the public and its own employees.

Because of the complex web of issues involved, it is doubtful that anyone, with the exception of a few senior managers, is completely knowledgeable of whole truth. It is a safe bet that most Freeport employees would never intentionally harm the environment or destroy a tribe of indigenous people. Yet, to date, Freeport has been, at the very least, in close proximity to thousands of deaths in Irian Jaya, the destruction of rain forests, the poisoning of a major river, and the financial support of a "democratic" dictator who maintains "consensus" by committing genocide in East Timor.

What is certain is that Freeport intends on extracting the $50 billion worth of gold and copper from the Irian Jaya mine. Not until the year 2026, when the mine is exhausted and Freeport retracts from Irian Jaya, will the truth be known. Have the lives of the Amunge and other tribes been improved by the mine as Freeport has suggested? Will the remote and lush environment of that Indonesian island survive the corporate footprint? Only after Jim Bob Moffett, recipient of $45 million in cash and stock during 1995,[14] and Freeport shareholders who have profited handsomely from the bullish actions of Moffett have long faded from view will we have the answers to these questions. Then it will be too late to tag any negative consequences on the perpetrator.

Freeport's narcissistic obsession with its image clearly manifests in the manipulation of public information. By limiting access to the truth and spinning off pseudo-environmental groups (Environmental Research Consortium of Louisiana and Crescent Technologies) to endorse its methods, Freeport persists in constructing a facade that is designed to calm the fears of investors and quell the protests of community, political, and environmental activists.

But the public relations campaign isn't working as well as was hoped. The narcissistic manipulations have created a pervasive distrust that prevents employees and the public from wholeheartedly accepting Freeport's story—even when it is the truth. The Irian Jaya natives, many now permanently distrustful of Freeport, continue to threaten operations at the mine. The violations of trust and honesty from the past continue to obstruct the company's future, even though many of those deceptive practices have been abandoned.

Evidence of mistrust of Freeport comes from the most unlikely of sources. Generally speaking, companies that earn the generous level of profit and return on investment that Freeport delivers are rarely criticized by the American business press. Nevertheless, *Business Week* and *The Wall Street Journal* have both praised Freeport for earnings, but thrown quizzical phrases in the company's direction. *Business Week* noted that while Freeport was sitting on a "fabulous treasure of mineral resources in Irian Jaya" it goes on to warn that "Freeport will have to do more to come to terms with them [Amunge]."[15]

WASTING ENERGY ON CONFLICT

Narcissistic organizations often find themselves in the same situation as Freeport. These companies expend every ounce of attainable energy to achieve success, only to find themselves sinking into unnecessary and, at times, devastating conflict. Through their manipulations of employees, suppliers, customers, and competitors, they eventually find themselves besieged on all fronts. The company must divert increasing resources to fighting battles that could have been avoided. In the worst of cases, the battles grow to consume the focus and finances of the organization, eventually destroying the health of the business.

The narcissistic organization sadly converts good intentions and hard work into escalating conflict and enduring pain. It harnesses the healthy needs of its employees and managers into a structure that is valueless and only directed by corporate profit. That collective force then plows through the community with disregard for anything that isn't profit-related. The welfare of humanity—the universal profit—becomes subservient to the self-serving interests of the corporation. Thus, the narcissistic organization succeeds and ultimately fails us all.

SIX

Corporate
Evangelists and
Chronic Campaigns

The scene on the television was serene. Sweeping aerial views of an African plain dotted with a loosely scattered herd of wildebeests casually grazing in seemingly endless grasslands. The older females tended the young, nosing these weaker members of the herd into protective custody. As I peered at this all-too-peaceful scene through the omniscient lens of the television camera flying somewhere overhead, there was a hint that something sinister was about to unfold.

Presently unheeded by the herd, a lioness gracefully stalked the herd. She slid among the tall grasses, quietly encircling the object of her next meal. Stepping forward then rolling backward and low, she slowly inched closer to the stray wildebeests that had carelessly wandered from the protection of the others.

Suddenly, she was seen. Eye to eye with her terrified prey, she sprung toward the herd. In flash, there was a roar, a cloud of dust, and an instantaneous race for survival. The lioness pursued the fleeing wildebeests, straining to overtake the slowest of the pack.

The herd seemed to move with the same mind and motion. They kept a seemingly premeditated formation as they fled across the grassy plains. No one dared look back. Each looked straight ahead, concentrating on the one that was before.

It was only a matter of time before the lioness had her prey. One of the slower members dropped dangerously behind the others and into the jaws of the determined predator. Still the herd ran on.

In panicked flight, they ran to stay ahead of an enemy who was no longer a threat. Charging forward as one, they mindlessly fled across the plain and over the unexpected edge of steep ravine. When the dust settled, well over half the herd had plunged to their deaths at the bottom of that ravine. Little did they know that the danger from which they fled was far less treacherous than the danger that lay before them.

FOLLOWING THE HERD

The day after I watched that grisly scene, I participated in a live radio interview in Seattle. My host, Dave Ross, spent the first fifteen minutes of the hour-long program interviewing me about my recent book on layoffs.* I commented on the current obsession in the business world with quarterly reports and how it leads companies to jeopardize their futures for a short-term gain in profit. With that, we went to the phones and Dave put a caller on the air.

The first caller was an economics professor from a local university who clearly disagreed with my last comment. "The last time I checked, seven days made a week, fifty-two weeks a year, ten years a decade," he said in a clipped, no-nonsense voice. "All a manager can do is raise profits today and hope that he can repeat himself seven times a week, fifty-two times a year. If he does, then he's been a success." According to this professor, corporate managers are perfectly justified in doing whatever it takes to raise profits in the current quarter. "Worry

*Corporate Executions, New York: AMACOM, 1995.

about today and let tomorrow take care of itself" was his advice.

After the show, I pondered what that caller had said. I was struck with how similar his theory of management was to the wildebeests I had seen the day before. One should do whatever he can to stay one step ahead of the lioness. That is success.

This theory would work if it weren't for the ravines—the unexpected changes in landscape that lie buried in the unknowable future. As it was for the wildebeests, a ravine can be more deadly than the immediate danger that stalks the company. Furthermore, only a few crippled companies fall to the lioness. The vast majority of causalities are from what lies ahead, not from the highly publicized demon behind.

Nevertheless, many companies follow the wildebeest theory of management. They flee danger by following the herd. With eyes fixed on the haunches of what is directly before them, they charge forward with limited foresight of what might lie ahead. Enveloped by the galloping herd, they stay in formation, each imitating the other without regard for strategy or destination. There is only panic and a herd mentality.

THE CORPORATE STAMPEDE

This is the corporate stampede. Companies line up, each blindly imitating the actions of the one before. Internally, employees line up, each mirroring the moves of the leader. No one dares break the formation or question the path. There is no time to think. The herd moves on and, lest you be trampled, you had better move, too. In this realm, rewards are meted by how fast one imitates, not innovates.

There are two distinct elements in the corporate stampede: an accepted, well-practiced method of action, and a "devil." It all starts when this devil appears in all of his horrific glory. Suddenly the organization must mobilize. The leader of the pack reacts and the rest of the loyal herd follows suit. In an instant, the company is in a terror-inspired, thoughtless flight. The speed builds and the momentum hurls the organization onward, away from its demonized enemy and toward an uncharted destiny. The devil is soon lost, but the organization rolls on as if once it is set in motion, its course cannot be changed.

Not a few senior managers have found their companies in just such choreographed panic. "Hold it!" they yell. "Where are we going and from what are we running?" they question, straining to be heard above the thunderous sound of thousands of employees all moving in rhythm.

The momentum of this stampede can be seductively hypnotic and stubbornly resistant to change. The manager who attempts to interrupt the flow, change the moves, and stop the imitations finds himself slamming into a seemingly impenetrable wall. But more often than not, fear and panic prevail, trampling those who stand in the way.

Sometimes there is a change in course. The old, deep ruts of the "way we do things around here" are paved over and a new course is laid. But even in these successes, the problem of stampedes isn't completely solved; it is merely abated for the time being. In time, the organization seems to ossify around the "new," sacred truth, and a new devil appears or is created by a management team eager to speed up the organization's pace. At first a trot, then a gallop, and before long, it is a full-scale, terror-driven, and mindless stampede.

Narcissism and the Stampede

Narcissistic leaders have become quite familiar with the stampede. They know the power behind thousands of employees running in the same direction. This power can be harnessed and used to advance the narcissist's own self-interests. It is as easy as yelling "fire!" in a crowded theater for the narcissist to create a stampede that quickly and forcibly moves the organization in his direction. If he is successful, not only can he create the originating "demon"; he can also be the savior that leads the herd to safety.

To be painfully clear, not all stampedes and not all corporate demons are the creations of narcissists. Both exist in a very real, day-to-day business world. At times the organization wanders so far off track that a stampede is the only hope for salvation. Predators do roam the corporate landscape and their ferocity should, for the preservation of life and limb, be respected.

THE HIJACK OF TOTAL QUALITY

However, in more than a few cases, corporate stampedes have the look and feel of a false alarm. For example, remember all the warnings several years back about the impending demise of American business if quality standards weren't improved? Remember how we compared the quality of our Japanese imports to the lumbering American counterparts of the day? The issue of quality started a number of legitimate stampedes in industries like the auto industry, where the lack of quality was diminishing revenues. Before we knew it, consultants were coming out of the woodwork, declaring every business in every industry a very sick patient whose only hope was total quality (or some other patented trademark name, like continuous improvement, zero defect, and so on). The stampede started in company after company, all rushing to buy the latest total quality training programs and allying themselves with Deming, Juran, or some other international guru of perfection. Companies spent millions of dollars competing for the Malcolm Baldrige award, an award that didn't even exist until the late 1980s.

What has happened to the quality movement? Where are all the fervent evangelists with their process analysis and Pareto charts? Many converts tell us that we reached quality nirvana—didn't you notice? Others, like University of Michigan researcher Kim Cameron, produce studies that show the total quality stampede was preempted by yet another stampede: downsizing/reengineering.[1]

Is it reasonable to believe that the quality movement actually improved corporate America's overall quality standards and saved us all from ruination? My personal experience, along with most studies on the topic, suggests otherwise. Quality standards were improved in a very limited group of manufacturing industries. The rest is proving to be nothing more than very expensive overkill.

In more than a few organizations, aspiring narcissists hijacked the quality movement for their own purposes. The narcissist needs a pulpit—a gimmick—a prophecy—to get the attention of the organization, and the quality movement was ripe with all of these. By simply comparing an organization's quality statistics to the zero-defect standard, the narcissist could make the case that quality was less than perfect. Drawing on the writings of prominent corporate evangelists, the narcissist could declare that improved quality was the solution to all corporate dilemmas. Then came the quality circles, continuous improvement teams, and piles and piles of graphs and statistics. It all looked very productive and, in many cases, achieved immediate albeit short-lived results. That was all the narcissist needed to advance his career a notch.

The tragedy of all this is that the quality movement genuinely had something productive to offer American business. In those cases when its efficacy wasn't usurped by an aspiring up-and-comer, lasting gains were realized. As often as not, however, total quality served the career purposes of a few and left the organization flailing about with cumbersome tools.

Corporate fads like total quality, reengineering, downsizing, managerial grid, management by objectives, and Hoshin planning, to name just a few, provide a fantastic vehicle for the narcissist who is going places. Where else could he find opportunity to lead a corporate-wide campaign? If a marketing or accounting or sales manager tried to expand his power beyond the defined confines of his department, it would be seen as a turf battle and staunchly resisted. A corporate campaign, on the other hand, is expected to cover all departments, and its leader gains tremendous visibility and power not otherwise attainable.

The narcissist isn't alone in riding the power wave of a corporate stampede. There is another group that has made a billion dollar industry off the creation and maintenance of these industrial panic attacks. Enter the management consultant.

MANAGEMENT CONSULTANTS

Management consultants can be an invaluable tool for the narcissist. They offer him a shortcut to credibility and prestige. The Ivy League MBAs and the long list of blue chip corporate clients create an aurora of expertise which the consultants sell to company. The narcissist, if attentive, learns that he can vicariously acquire some of their cache and moxie simply by being the one to introduce the consultants to the organization.

The consultants can fill some pressing needs for the narcissist. Because he lacks a sense of self, the narcissist doesn't trust the validity of his own ideas. The management consultant, carrying the prestigious firm name with him, offers validation to those ideas. It is much easier to convince a skeptical board of directors by waving a report from McKinsey or Arthur Andersen than it is to offer a rather simple: "I think it will work. Really."

The consultant also provides an instant scapegoat should things go wrong. If the project starts to head south, the narcissist need only to distance himself from the project and start blaming the consultant. The game of "the consultant made me do it" has been played by more than a few corporate managers attempting serious career damage control. For the narcissist, scapegoats are important and necessary elements for any undertaking.

And, of course, consultants are often the best way to start a stampede. They offer the ability to diagnose the company, prescribe the program that will fix the problem, administer that program, and, after it is all over, conduct the follow-up study that declares the program a success. The first job of most consultants is to provide an analysis that is so powerfully convincing, it starts the stampede in their direction.

Management consultants are notorious for developing their pet diagnoses and organizational elixirs. They practice these cures until they develop into an art form and, in recent times, have started patenting the associated buzzwords. Andersen Consulting, for one, has laid claim to the ubiquitous phrase "change management." CSC/Index, Inc., has home-steaded the term "business reengineering." Not to be outdone by a competitor, McKinsey & Co. calls the same thing "business process redesign" and Coopers & Lybrand sells it as "breakpoint business process reengineering." All of these programs have one major objective: to start a reengineering-reorganizing-downsizing stampede with their clients.

If the narcissist plays the consultant well, he can convince the organization that it has a problem it didn't know it had and then heroically offer the solution. Since a major part of any management consulting engagement is feeding the client the right information and terminology, the narcissist is coached by experts on how to sell the consultant's analysis and solution to the organization. It is a basic tenet of successful management consulting: Make the client look good. If all goes well, the narcissist looks like a brilliant visionary who saved the company from disaster.

Many a narcissist has used management consultants as a personal public relations firm. Not only do the consultants carefully guard his self-interest within the company; they are often well-connected to other organizations in the same industry. They are in a unique position to promote the client to other companies and executives. One consultant, David Nadler of Delta Consulting, even went so far as to co-author a book with his client, David Kearns, CEO of Xerox, which extolled the virtues of Delta's consulting services and the expert management skills of Xerox senior management. Some of the best public relations firms in the country couldn't have dished up better publicity.

The book is titled *Prophets in the Dark*, and inside the front cover the first sentence reads: "A great American success story!" While the jacket claims the book chronicles how Xerox reinvented itself and beat back the Japanese, it reads more like the self-congratulatory diary of two men, one a CEO and the other a management consultant. It describes in detail how Nadler helped Kearns implement the tools of total quality throughout the Xerox organization.

Contrary to the flattering picture the book paints of their work at Xerox, the company posted a $1 billion loss and laid off 10,000 employees while the book was still on bookstore shelves. Clearly, Kearns and Nadler were trying very hard to put a positive spin on a dire situation.[2]

The problem is not that consultants publicize the workings of their clients; after all, much of any consultant's expertise is based on previous experience with clients. It is that some managers hire consultants strictly for what the consultant can do for their career. In my own consulting practice and that of many of my colleagues, we have noticed a dramatic increase in the number of inquiries from managers who will buy the services of any consultant that will make them look good. They are not interested in buying the consultant's objective analysis; rather, what they want is someone who will agree with their predetermined conclusions; that agreement inevitably will put them in the best possible light and protect their managerial power base. Of course, no one ever says these things directly, but the message is nonetheless clear.

Because management consulting is much like alternative medicine—there are few, if any, scientific studies to back up claims—some practitioners are willing to sell just about anything to a client who will buy it. Unless blatant fraud is involved, the consultant needn't worry about malpractice claims. There is no license or governing agency that sets standards of competence or certifies practitioners. This has, unfortunately, opened the door to an unholy alliance between some ambitious consultants and aspiring corporate narcissists. Some companies are paying millions of dollars every year for this relationship.

MANAGEMENT MOVEMENTS DISTORTED

Founders of business movements like total quality and reengineering are often dismayed at how their original concepts are distorted as the movement progresses. Michael Hammer, for example, has repeatedly expressed frustration with the fact that his original ideas in *Reengineering the Corporation* have been badly misconstrued by consultants and companies who have labeled virtually every major corporate action as "reengineering." One only need pick up one of the several hundred books on total quality to realize that the term has become so all inclusive, it is now rendered meaningless.

Great corporate thinkers and philosophers have pondered the derailing of these and other business movements. Some have suggested these movements were nothing more than trendy fads to begin with. Others seem to think that corporate America has assimilated them into everyday business. Few, if any, have been willing to acknowledge that there is a small group of managers who are intentionally disemboweling these programs and using them for their own self-serving purposes. They take a basic truth and mold it into a chariot that carries them to the forefront of organizational power and politics, eventually discarding the program, leaving it to wither and die. The decline of total quality, reengineering, management by objectives, and many other movements has little to do with their inapplicability or assimilation into the organizational landscape. Rather, it is because their champions were never committed to the basic principles or outcomes, and used the program to advance their personal standing in the organization.

Section 3

BEYOND NARCISSISM

SEVEN

The Organization as Reluctant Host

As challenging a problem as corporate narcissism is, there is a relatively simple and straightforward solution: Create an organizational environment that doesn't tolerate extreme narcissistic behavior.

There is little hope of changing the business practices of the narcissist. As we've seen, the problems of this overly ambitious manager go far beyond just the corporate setting, and it would be foolish to try to fix those problems within the parameters of business. Psychotherapists, counselors, and ministers (not to mention more than a few spouses) spend years trying to help narcissists change their behavior and understand the roots of their overwhelming needs. Patching the problem with the usual corporate quick fix of routing an article, recommending a book, or holding a training session does little more than raise awareness of the problem. The real solution lies not in changing the narcissist but in changing the environment that allows the narcissist to thrive.

ORGANIZATIONAL SELF-AWARENESS

The first and most important step is what management consultant Elise Walton has called organizational "identity and self-awareness."[1] Because of the size and complexity of most organizations, very few truly understand what they do best. Operations may spread across many continents and involve any number of processes and departments. Grasping the whole can be extremely difficult, and without that gestalt, the core competencies of the organization can remain hidden.

Nevertheless, one of the key frontline defenses against organizational narcissism is a confident and collective knowledge of what the organization does best. When that knowledge permeates the organization, it is less vulnerable to those who would attempt to steer it away from those competencies for their personal gain. Ever-present political structures and alliances become subservient to fulfilling those key objectives. If a manager is to build an empire and climb the corporate ladder, he must do so by enhancing the organization's ability to deliver. Departments and programs that offer little tangible gain become quickly and easily identifiable. Often, they self-destruct because the associated managers assess the irrelevance of their own endeavors.

UNCOVERING THE CORE

The struggle to identify and grasp the core competencies of an organization is illustrated by the experience of a large utility company on the West Coast. For years the company had operated a fossil fuel power plant in a small town that was several hundred miles from the company's general offices. For over forty years the power plant had run the same way it did on its first day of operation. Processes and jobs were standardized in ironclad tradition. Very little had changed at the plant, including the employee and management roster.

The utility company would have left the mammoth consortium of smokestacks and coal mountains to run itself, had it not been for one fact: The plant's reliability had slowly been diminishing to an all-time low of 50 percent. While no power plant can enjoy 100 percent reliability, due to refueling and maintenance operations, a half-on, half-off operation is not only inefficient, it virtually doubles the cost of the power it does produce.

Dan Sinclair was the manager tapped on the shoulder to replace the retiring career-long manager of the plant. Dan, a thirty-something manager of a geothermal power plant, knew little about the operation of a fossil fuel plant despite his engineering background. There was nothing sexy about a fossil plant; it was old technology that few in the power industry cared about, and Dan worried that by association, his new assignment might take the gleam off his career, too.

Dan's first day at the plant was truly a step back in time. Not only was he one of the youngest managers at the plant— the plant itself reeked of the 1950s. The black-and-white asphalt tile hallways reminded him of elementary school. The office doors—a luxury of the precubicle era—sported frosted glass windows behind which shadowy figures hunched over large oak desks. Even the phone system maintained the bygone greeting of a manual switchboard.

One of Dan's first experiences at the plant was a morning staff meeting of the top plant managers. The meeting was stilted and agenda-driven. Nobody contributed extemporaneously, and everything seemed scripted with an air of practiced recitation. Much to Dan's surprise, no one would make eye contact with him, and the air was thick with tension. "My God," he thought, "there must have been a fatality on the job last night."

The only sound was the creaking of slatted wooden chairs and the clinking of coffee cups into their pre-mug saucers. As the meeting ground forward and the managers seemed to squirm anxiously, one man finally addressed Dan directly: "Mr. Sinclair, is there a policy change you haven't told us about?"

Dan thought for a moment. Policy change? I just walked into the building. He said deliberately, "Not from me."

The puzzled manager checked the other faces for support and then spurted out, "Mr. Sinclair, it has been a policy at the power plant that all general foremen and above wear a tie everyday. You don't have on a tie."

Dan hadn't yet grasped the situation he had taken on. Ties were just the tip of the misbegotten iceberg of trivia and distraction that had slowly taken the place of real business issues at the plant. His first and most important job at Moss Cove would be to refocus the plant on what mattered most: the production of reliable power.

Dan told those at the staff meeting that they would spend the next day walking the plant. The staff should wear something comfortable and appropriate for crawling over rusty power generators. "That means," he joked, "leave the ties at home."

The next day, the staff appeared in khaki pants and buttoned-up short-sleeve shirts. As it turned out, this was the plant's ordained uniform for managers on "hands-on" days.

The third day, Dan had several local media interviews planned and showed up at morning staff meeting wearing a suit and tie. Once again, the air was vibrating with anxiety: No one had worn a tie.

Dan, beginning to realize depth of the problem that ties represented, started the first of many changes aimed at focusing the organization on critical factors. "Look," he said, "I came today dressed to do what I need to do. If you need a new policy, okay, here it is: Dress for what your job requires. Period."

As time went on, Dan discovered that many of the people at Moss Cove were real pros. They knew their individual jobs with a precision that comes only from years of practice. Unfortunately, these skilled employees were entrenched in a very hierarchical, regimented organization that compartmentalized jobs and rarely provided the opportunity for creative cross-pollination among differing functions. Employees were extremely loyal to their own department managers and saw no reason to cross territorial lines that separated each manager's domain.

There were other signs that signaled not all was well within the antiseptic hallways of that plant. Most notably, during the previous year, the 250 bargaining unit employees of the plant had filed 110 formal grievances regarding management practices at the plant. Employees kept a very low profile, risked nothing, and never offered ideas, even when upper management invited them. Generally speaking, success was defined as "not getting in trouble."

Instilling a Sense of Common Mission

About four months after his arrival, Dan felt compelled to start dealing with the underlying problems that were dragging down plant reliability and making Moss Cove a regimented and generally miserable place to work. The first job was to instill a sense of common mission throughout the organization.

Dan started a series of Tuesday evening meetings with the fourteen department managers and general foremen. Over dinner, he asked each of the managers to talk about the problems and successes of their departments. At first the meetings were nothing more than managerial beauty pageants where everyone trotted out their best stories and most remarkable victories. Over several months, however, the meetings began to become more honest. Slowly and very carefully the managers began admitting to the problems they were encountering and asking for advice from Dan and the other managers.

After a dozen or so of these meetings, Dan started a structured process of determining the core competencies of the plant. The discussions were guided by questions like, "Why does the Moss Cove plant exist?" "Who are our customers?" "Who is dependent upon us and why?" and finally, "What do we do best?"

The first to venture answers to these questions offered nothing more than corporate speak—formula answers straight from the plant's list of 60 performance objectives. After a few meetings of wading through reams of documents, a barrage of objectives, and stacks of flipcharts, the group was able to narrow its focus onto four agreed-upon objectives for the plant. Not surprisingly, plant reliability was at the top of that list.

Dan challenged the group to come up with what they

thought was the highest possible reliability rating for the plant—what Dan called "a medal of honor rating." After a few weeks of study and calculations by the engineering department, the group agreed that 62 percent was the top shelf of reliability.

Suspecting that number was too low, Dan invested a few thousand dollars in buying national statistics for fossil fuel plants. Overall, the average reliability rating was in the mid-sixties, with the best performing plants reaching 75 percent. At the next meeting Dan greeted the group with a big 75 written on a flipchart. He remembers hearing audible gasps in the room.

"Can't be done," seemed to be the consensus. The group fired back at Dan with all the reasons—many of them valid—why the plant couldn't meet the 75 percent goal. After things settled down, Dan pushed the group to think. "Imagine for a minute that 75 percent reliability were possible. What would it take to make it happen?"

That one question drove the next batch of Tuesday night meetings. The group began homing in on what drives the Moss Cove plant reliability. The meetings were frustrating, labor intensive, and highly educational. If 75 percent were to be a reality, no stone could remain unturned and no aspect of the plant could go unexamined. Two paths emerged from their work.

The first path concerned hardware engineering and maintenance. The group identified a number of areas where the engineering department and maintenance teams weren't cooperating and were, at times, defeating each other's efforts. With time, some reorganization, and capital spending to update equipment, the hardware issues could be resolved.

The second path involved upgrading the manner in which all employees worked together (or didn't, as was often the case). The group decided what the plant needed was a totally revised organizational chart. Cross-functional teams seemed to be the answer to many of the problems that were contributing to reliability deterioration. After considerable discussion and input from the union, the plant began an overhaul of the organization chart, including revamping the compensation program to reward managers and employees for team participation.

Meeting the Goal

Within a year, the plant had reached a reliability of 63 percent—an improvement, but still short of the goal. As luck would have it, this was the same year that a plant overhaul was scheduled. Because of heavy demands placed on the power plant generators, they had to be overhauled and sometimes replaced every ten years. An overhaul was a painful task that always went over-schedule and over-budget. Since the overhaul usually occurred in the late fall, it often extended into the Christmas holidays and forced the staff to continue working around the clock through the holiday season. In the past, overhauls were characterized by high tension, blame, and even a few fistfights.

The management group, now an emerging team, vowed to make this the best overhaul it could be and to use some of the teamwork they had created at their session to do it. To start, they opened up the process and invited suggestions for improvement from all employees. Teams at all levels were involved in planning the overhaul. The management team made sure that everyone knew that the goal was to finish on time and on cost with a unit that was reliable and efficient. Blaming someone else would not be tolerated.

For the first time in anyone's memory, there was a sense of excitement and challenge about the overhaul. Amazingly, the plant pulled off the overhaul on schedule and under budget. Better still, everyone was at home for the holidays. It was a landmark event that proved to everyone the value of the new management style.

Within three years, the plant achieved a sustained reliability of 75 percent. Dan threw a spectacular celebration, replete with brass bands and barbecue. The company CEO even came down and personally congratulated each of the teams for their unprecedented accomplishments.

The success at Moss Cove illustrates the power of identifying and leveraging the core competencies of an organization.
By deciding what is most important to the business and then
restructuring the organization to fulfill those clearly understood objectives, Moss Cove was able to build momentum that
eventually exceeded the expectations of its own staff.

It is also of no small consequence that the process of
identifying core competencies forced the organization to break
down the walls of territorialism that had been established for
decades. By making the organization an open book, there was
no place for the manager whose objectives weren't in sync
with the organization's overall direction. Those who were pulling in a different direction eventually became obvious anoma-
lies.

LEVERAGING COMPETENCIES

Once the organization has completed the process of identifying and leveraging its core competencies, steps must be taken
to insure this information is always present at every level in
the organization. There are four key areas where management
can insure that core competencies remain central to the organizations activities. These areas are:

1. Hiring and promoting employees
2. Continuous learning and training
3. Performance evaluation and management
4. Honest communications

EMPLOYEE HIRING AND PROMOTION

One of the best ways to ensure that organizational core competencies are maintained throughout the organization is to
give those competencies a primary role in the hiring of new
employees and the promotion of existing employees. By selecting employees whose skills complement the core competencies, management ensures that the organization grows along

the veins of its strengths. It also sends a living message throughout the company of the organization's priorities. Employees always pay close attention to who is hired or promoted and, more importantly, why.

There are a variety of techniques that are useful in making solid employment decisions, and a complete discussion of all is obviously beyond the scope of this book. There is one technique, however, that is simple, straightforward, and almost foolproof. It is the technique of the situational interview.

Situational interviews are nothing more than asking a job candidate to recount actual, on-the-job experiences that relate to a particular trait or competency. In contrast, the usual job interview is heavily based on hypothetical questions that ask the candidate what he might do in a certain situation. The situational interview does not allow hypothetical questions or answers; it forces the candidate to give specific, behavioral details of how he handled the given situation.

For example, to determine how a candidate has solved conflicts in the past, the interviewer might ask, "Tell me, in as much detail as possible, about an actual situation in your past where on-the-job-conflict was involved. Specifically, how did you handle the situation? What did you do to resolve the situation and what was the final outcome?"

A determined situational interviewer will kindly guide the candidate back to behavioral specifics should he slip into hypotheticals, as most of us are wont to do in an interview. By pushing the candidate to give only actual facts of past behavior, the interviewer is making it very difficult for the candidate to falsify details or "clean-up" his answer. It is extremely difficult, if not impossible, for a candidate to consistently lie about specifics of his own behavior. All candidates have the desire to present themselves in the best light, and a strict situational interview is more likely to uncover their true competencies. By structuring these situations around organizational core competencies, the interviewer can more accurately assess the candidate's fit within the organization and its culture.

Why is situational interviewing important in the battle against corporate narcissism? To begin with, a situational interview is extremely difficult for the narcissist who is trying to sell his image. Most narcissists will make the mistake of presenting themselves as more than what they really are. When pushed by the situational interviewer for specific facts about the situation, the narcissist is forced to retreat into vague generalities. If the candidate is attempting to take credit for the work of others, another common narcissistic tactic, he is unable to recite accurate and believable details.

It is also very common for narcissists to reveal themselves in a situational interview. Most narcissists are very proud of their strategic climb to power and success. Given the opportunity and a willing ear, they will often recount their manipulations with surprising truthfulness, especially if they think such tactics will win them a better position.

The same situational technique can be helpful in determining promotions. By examining a candidate's past record through the situational lens, one must continually ask, "Exactly how were these results attained?" Recommendations from past supervisors and peers can be given similar treatment: "Can you give me some specific details about how he accomplished this job?"

TRANSFORMATION THROUGH TRAINING

Training is one of the most powerful techniques for driving core competence throughout the organization. Carefully designed training can give the employee a "big picture" view of the company and its services that is otherwise impossible to get through the narrow confines of a single job. This kind of knowledge is necessary for employees to then figure out what aspects of their own jobs contribute and enhance these organizational competencies. One company, Mervyn's Department Stores, has done an exceptional job of training employees on core competencies.

TRAINING CORE COMPETENCIES

If you cross the Bay from San Francisco and head south, you will eventually come upon a rather unremarkable industrial park nestled next to a semi-birdless bird sanctuary at the foot of the San Mateo Bridge. The surroundings may not grab you, but what is happening inside those low slung, pre-fabricated warehouses will. This is the corporate home for Mervyn's, a 4.5 billion dollar, 265 store retailer that is self-described as somewhere between a discounter (Wal-Mart) and a department store (Macy's). Training is transforming this company and, according to its senior officers, making a real difference in the bottom line.

Part of the highly successful Dayton Hudson empire of retail since 1977, the last ten years have been bittersweet for the California-based chain. Rapid expansion through the decade of the 1980s more than tripled the number of stores and thrust the company out of the realm of a small, family-owned department store to that of a national retailer. Going into the 1990s the company's distribution and buying systems were struggling to keep up with the growth. In an industry where execution is everything, the effect was clear: same-store sales began declining. To add even more pain, Mervyn's found itself in what had previously been thought impossible—a recession in California, where 45 percent of its stores are located. Mervyn's management began to grasp for answers as Dayton-Hudson turned up the heat.

Today, things are definitely changing at Mervyn's, and the training department is helping to lead the charge. The training that is helping to turn around this 45-year-old retailer is fashionably named "Mervyn's University." Despite the fact that this "university" has all the trappings—a campus, faculty, alumni, and, yes, collegiate sweatshirts—it is anything but the traditional ivory tower. Mervyn's University is a place where corporate theorists and hard-line retailers meet with what is often seen as the turning point of their Mervyn's careers.

What makes Mervyn's University (MU) so transformational isn't so much in its *content* but in the *experience* it offers. The program sprouted in the late 1980s, not in the hothouses of experienced trainers and course designers, but in the rocky ground of the front line: the retail store. Store managers and district managers began to see a disturbing trend of high turnover as manager after manager drowned in the increasingly treacherous waters of retail for lack of skills to do the job. It was here that the program was originally developed by district managers determined to develop their people and help them manage their business. Those "hands-on" roots are what continue to nourish the program and push it past being just a training program to being a career-altering experience.

Area Manager in Training Program

MU is a collection of experientially based training programs, the cornerstone of which is the Area Manager in Training Program. This program lasts for ten weeks and includes both on-the-job training and classroom instruction. There are four phases, each of which has specific performance measures which must be satisfied before the trainee can progress to the next phase.

During one phase of program, the trainees are led through training modules on performance management, leadership, merchandise presentation, and managing for "in-stock." The classes are led by a team of two managers from the stores who have accepted a rotational position as an MU instructor. The week focuses heavily on application back on the job and culminates in the students' presentation of a sales plan, shortage reduction plan, and merchandise presentation or "block" plan before a team of store managers who scrutinize every detail with persistent questioning after the presentation.

By the end of the program, the trainees must pass short answer and essay examinations, and presentations. During the last day, each trainee is met with individually for feedback about his performance throughout the week. The feedback consists of test scores and notations that the trainers have written about the trainees during the week and is structured so that everyone gets information on their strengths and development needs. By the time the trainees board a plane for the trip home, they know exactly where they stand.

Throughout the program, especially during the class-room phase, emotions run high. There is a "boot camp" intensity that pushes the group of trainees forward and *together*. They are keenly aware of the consequences of not passing and that seems to drive, not competitiveness, but a strong sense of team, or "partnering" as it is called in the Mervyn's culture. In fact, teamwork is so important in this culture that a one-upmanship, I'm-in-this-to-win-at-any-cost is a quick way to fail. According to John Irvin, senior vice president and general merchandise manager, "the two objectives of the program are to connect with the customer and connect with each other."

The trainees suggest an added benefit of attending the program. Many of the "new profile" hires have worked in retail for many years and report never having had such thorough training before. The fact that the company spends time and money to prepare them for the job shows a strong commitment to the employee *and* a high expectation of performance. Robyn Martinez, a recent graduate of the program and sixteen-year veteran of retailing, said "Mervyn's University shows you that they care about your success in the job."

The evidence of return on investment in Mervyn's University is popping up everywhere. Sandy Salyer, Vice President of Public Affairs and a twenty-year Mervyn's employee, noted "I could tell when I walked through the department of a graduate of Mervyn's University. It looked different. Suddenly, they were talking about the fundamentals of their business with you." That was a major change from the "earn while you learn," on-the-job training that existed when she joined the company in 1975. "When I became an officer, I looked around and realized that many people were failing at their jobs simply because they didn't have the right training. I even began to wonder if the same thing might happen to me."[2]

Managing the Pipeline

Recently, I attended a day-long module of the Merchandising Team program. The day was called "Managing the Pipeline" and was designed to raise an awareness of what happens to merchandise as it flows down the "pipeline" from vendor through the distribution center and on to the store and customer. What I saw bore little resemblance to the traditional training classroom with which I was familiar. I was astounded at how much learning appeared to be taking place.

As I pulled into the parking lot of the Milpitas, California, strip mall, the fog was just beginning to lift. I could see a huddled group of fifteen or so smartly dressed people waiting at the side door. Since it was several hours before the store opened, it was clear that these were not customers or store employees. These were the merchants—swathed in their fashionably chic outfits—waiting with the usual time urgency of a merchant.

In the world of retail, merchants and store managers are two different lots. Merchants are those within the company who make the decisions about what merchandise the company will buy. They are hired for their understanding of the market and their aesthetic sensibility. Merchants can become celebrated "stars" within the company. A good buying decision can have enormous financial benefits for the company and create a loyal following among customers. On the other hand, store managers are a more practical type and are probably best likened to "heroes," in all their martyred glory. They are heroes in that they can make or break a good buying decision just by where they display the merchandise or how they handle customers and martyrs in that they are ever mindful of the long hours and sacrifice they must endure to keep the store open long after the merchants have gone home. Although both merchants and store managers have tremendous impact on each other, they are usually housed in different locations, and their paths rarely cross. On this day, the merchants would have an opportunity to see firsthand just how their decisions can affect the stores.

After the door was unlocked, the group was quickly divided into teams according to the department with which the merchant worked. Then the teams were sent to the store's loading dock to begin the process of unloading boxes and racks off the truck. As if they had discovered some hidden treasure the insights immediately began flowing.

"They put one of my wallets in a box filled with fleece. No wonder so many wallets get lost!"

"These shirts are a flat program. Why have they put them on hangers?"

"This store should have never gotten this many of this style belt!"

As they moved from the loading dock to the sales floor, the usual mindless chatter was regularly punctuated with exclamations. There wasn't enough room on a fixture for all the dresses. How was it that all the signs in one department were wrong? This merchandise program should be right on the high-traffic isle!

After several hours of moving merchandise from the truck to the fixture in a "floor ready" condition, the group reconvened in the store's training room. As the facilitator asked each team to list on a flipchart all of the issues that they had discovered, the most common word that seemed to float above each of the small groups was "they." *They* didn't ship the right merchandise. *They* didn't use the right hangers. *They* sent the wrong signs. *They* didn't follow the block plan.

Then the facilitator skillfully prodded each group to also list what "we," not "they," could do to solve the issues listed. With equal fervor, the groups began generating laundry lists of what could be done to prevent many of these problems. By the end of the session, hardly a person present didn't have a full plate of action items. The "they's" had become "me."

The afternoon was something of a repeat of the morning, but this time at the local distribution center. Here each of the teams was assigned to a guide—someone who normally works with that department's merchandise. The distribution center rarely gets a chance to show the merchants how their buying decisions dramatically affect the efficiency of processing. It was clear we were about to see just that. The guide wryly said, "I've put aside a few boxes of your merchandise that might interest you."

With that she pushed open the double doors, and we were nearly sucked into a room that must have been the size of two football fields. The heavy din of all the conveyors muddled the exclamations as the group eyed with amazement the almost Disneyland quality of the distribution center. High-speed conveyors dipped and sailed like roller-coaster tracks whisking boxes from one station to the next. Laser scanners nabbed boxes, reading in a flash their contents and destination. With uncanny accuracy, fingerlike projections reached out and pushed those same boxes at the just the right time onto yet another conveyor that ended in the cavern of a semi-trailer bound for a particular store. It was all complex and amazingly precise. Judging from the awestruck faces of the merchants I was with, it was clear that they had no idea so much was involved in dividing and packaging materials for the stores. What they would soon learn was that their buying decisions and vendor negotiations were critical to this operation.

First there was the merchandise that arrived in boxes covered with strapping that was strong enough to lift a tank—strong enough to delay opening the hundreds of boxes by a couple of days. Then there were the jeans whose box said one size, plastic wrapping said another, and inseam label, still another size. We moved on to the sweatshirts, which were individually packed in plastic and then grouped in fives and double wrapped in plastic, all of which had to be stripped from the merchandise before it could be sorted. The inventory analyst in our group shook his head and said, "they (the manufacturer) are worried that if their container fell off the ship, all this plastic is what will save the merchandise." Everyone laughed at the absurdity.

At the end of the day, the teams met back to debrief what they had learned. Once again the list was legion. Many, if not all, of the problems they had encountered throughout the day could be solved by a simple phone call or negotiation at the time of purchase. By understanding the "pipeline," they had learned some valuable lessons about what they could do improve the efficiency with which merchandise flowed through system. Since every time the merchandise is handled it is delayed and that subsequently costs money, the results of the day were profitable.

The merchants were amazed at how quickly the day had gone by. That, in and of itself, is noteworthy. Being a merchant is as invigorating and demanding as playing a slot machine. You make a decision and pull the handle. Then you watch as the numbers change. You may pull the handle with "pocket T-shirts" and win big as they sell out or you may pull the handle with Lycra shorts and come up flat with extra mark downs and clearance merchandise. Anyway you look at it, there is a fast-paced element of chance in the job. Getting merchants to leave the control of their desks for a whole day takes a major effort. To have them actually appreciate the loss of that day from the job is nothing short of miraculous.

Focusing on Improvement

Probably the most remarkable effect of MU on the organization is how it is influencing senior management. One recent example is when the MU staff began developing a program that was centered on the profile of the Mervyn's customer. According to Carolyn Yates, manager of program development, that's when real problems arose. There was a definite opinion about who the customer was—but that picture depended on whom you talked to. When the training staff put it all together, nobody could agree on the fine-tuned version. That prompted Yates's boss to approach senior management to resolve the issue. First, there had to be agreement before there could be training.

Yates characterizes the MU classroom as a place for dialogue. She sees it as an ever evolving forum where ideas are experienced, learned, and improved. Her staff of course designers have the ongoing responsibility to keep up with that dialogue and create an experiential learning environment that focuses on continuous improvement. She says they do not create change; rather, MU provides a place where change can be discussed. But it is clear that MU, through dialogue, is creating its own wake of change.

The case of Mervyn's is one of an organization that is simultaneously discovering itself and disseminating that knowledge throughout the organization. Because an organization is never static, the process is continuous. Like Mervyn's, healthy organizations must make learning a continuous process that lives within the organization's structure.

Most importantly, Mervyn's University is strengthening the true "corporate" bond among its managers and employees. The program instills a strong sense of collective ownership in the company and makes the organization's culture resistant to those who would abuse it for personal gain. By empowering all new managers with a working knowledge of departments throughout the organization and encouraging cross-functional dialogue, narcissistic territorial boundaries are extremely difficult to erect.

PERFORMANCE EVALUATION AND MANAGEMENT

Another important weapon in the war against corporate narcissism is the performance appraisal. In most organizations the appraisal is a yearly occurrence that is dreaded by supervisors and employees alike. The list for postponing or avoiding performance reviews is long and varied. Suffice it to say that the performance review is among the most disliked of all corporate obligations.

But the timely and honest performance review is absolutely critical to the organization's health. It is the one dedicated moment each year where a supervisor and employee are forced to deal with *how* an employee does his job. As we have seen, the seeds of the narcissistic culture lie in the "how."

One of the more effective methods for honestly dealing with the "how" is a 360° performance review. A 360° review is one that encompasses the full circle of an employee's job by collecting data from peers, subordinates, and the supervisor. Some more aggressive 360° reviews even include feedback from customers, vendors, and other internal departments.

Although the 360° performance review requires special care, if used properly it can be a forceful tool in drawing a complete picture of an employee's performance. As opposed to the traditional supervisory review, the feedback from peers and subordinates in a 360° performance review can help identify the methods an employee uses to accomplish goals— methods that may have otherwise remained hidden from the supervisor's limited perspective. The 360° review makes it more difficult for a narcissist to protect those enablers who help him accomplish his personal objectives but do so at the organization's expense.

For the performance review to be effective, it must become something of a sacred event within the organization. Reviews must be timely, thoughtful, and thorough. If it is a 360° review, contributors must be guaranteed protection from retaliation or, if possible, anonymity. All this takes a considerable amount of time and effort on the part of a management team. From the top down, managers must be rewarded for fulfilling these objectives. Otherwise, the performance review becomes just another human resource form that is a bureaucratic nightmare to administer.

TO TELL THE TRUTH

Moving beyond the culture corporate of narcissism demands a reverence for truth. Nothing but the simple, honest truth. Not the spin, not the "internal" sales pitch, not the public relations version. If the corporate obsession with dressed-up, narcissistic image is to be diminished, the organization must demand nothing short of the whole truth from both managers and employees. For many companies today, this simple idea is amazingly radical.

MORE THAN ONE VERSION OF THE TRUTH

A few years ago I ran headlong into this issue when I consulted with a nonprofit organization. The agency was in

big trouble when I took on the job. The former agency director, a charming and well-liked public figure, had been
ousted through a torrent of ill-planned interventions by the
president of the board of directors. Furious at having been
fired from *her* agency—the agency she had built from a one-
person office—she took her story to the local media, to the
agency donors, and, worst of all, to the courts. She proclaimed that she had been bullied out of her job by a board
of directors that was more concerned about the social status
that comes from being on a charity board than they were
the services provided by the agency. Not one penny, she
said, had been raised by the board and further, none of the
board members had given the required donation of several
thousand dollars.

I entered the scene the morning after the newly fired
director was locked out of the office. The office was in worse
shape than I had imagined. In the confusion of the previous
evening, files had been removed from the office, ledgers had
been altered, and mailing lists had been destroyed. What
was left was a complete shambles. In the weeks that followed, I concentrated on pulling the staff together and trying
to reorganize the office. Although my specialty isn't office
management, I was forced to spend the better part of a
month reassembling the basic business processes.

Within just a few days it became clear to me that the
former director had been right about a number of things. In
fact, she had understated the severity of a few of them.
Board members, many of whom had their own keys to the
office, would come in unannounced and proceed to interrupt daily business to discuss whatever was on their mind,
like sending this "very important" and "well-connected"
person literature on the agency or their latest brainstorm for
a charity gala. They were undoubtedly trying to be helpful
but their constant interruptions created chaos for the staff.

Board members felt free to involve themselves in all
areas of the operation, from minute details like cleaning the
rest room to larger issues like firing personnel and relocating
offices. It was not uncommon for me, an outside consultant,
to be pulled aside and told things like, "Was I aware that

this particular staff person wasn't very well liked by the board? The board would appreciate it if I would find the necessary reasons to fire him."

The board president was the worst of all. Many times he would call and demand that the entire staff drop whatever they had planned to meet with him at his convenience (often after the staff had put in an eight-hour day) or to put together an emergency mailing or to start yet another phone campaign. Always, "no" was not an acceptable answer.

Halfway through my agreed-upon work with the agency, I decided to terminate the job. I was defeated and frustrated. I, too, began to feel anger when board members, many of whom had been personal friends, walked into the office. I had reached the limit of what good I could do.

When I met with the board president to discuss my leaving, I prepared a memo outlining some of my reasons for terminating early. I listed as carefully as I could all the things I thought should be changed, including the role of the board in managing the agency. As with most nonprofit agencies, I suggested that the board limit its activities to board oversight and fundraising, and leave the day-to-day operations to the agency management. Little did I know my memo was a virtual carbon copy of the memo the former director had written before being fired.

The president and I discussed the memo briefly as his distinguished profile grew fiery red against the backdrop of his neatly cropped gray hair. He leaned forward on the desk, shifting his weight onto his hands, which were propped on the desktop like a wildcat before the attack. He looked directly at me and said, "There are many versions of the truth, and frankly, I don't like yours." With that he demanded that I destroy all copies of this memo and write another memo that politely excused me from working with the agency. Did I not know that they were embroiled in a lawsuit over these very same matters? For God's sake, this could be used as evidence for the other side!

But it was the obvious truth. Everyone who worked at the agency and most of the board members knew it. In the narcissistic organization, however, truth is irrelevant. What counts is the spin, the version of truth that makes the organization look the best. If the truth is unpleasant, as it was at the agency, then it is heresy and must be hidden.

Valuing the Truth

One of the most important steps in moving beyond the culture of narcissism starts with valuing the truth. Not the dressed-up version, but the reality of business. Not the story that makes me look clean, and defenseless Joe the scapegoat, but the one that admits failure where and with whom it happened.

Hand-in-glove with valuing the truth is protecting those who tell it. Failure is a normal and expected part of being human. All managers and all companies fail at some time. When the company cuts off those who tell of the failure, or worse, those who admit to failing, it sends a powerful message that the truth is not important and that ugly truths should be avoided at all costs. Once this happens, counterfeit presses start rolling, and the truth becomes cloaked.

The organization that is able to move beyond the false beauty of hiding unpleasant truths is the organization that knows its capabilities and capitalizes on them. Failure has as much, if not more, informational value as success. Employees who are supported not just when they shine, but also when they occasionally slip, are wedded to the company. As a result, they are willing to return that loyalty and support when the company falters and needs a little extra help.

How to Work in the Narcissistic Organization

Enduring change demands commitment from top management. Without the direct involvement of the senior team, the culture of the organization will not change. Only highly visible, new behaviors emanating from the top steer the organization toward freedom from narcissistic practices.

IT STARTS AT THE TOP

Carolyn and I sat in the trendy nouvelle-Polynesian-California-cuisine restaurant making the usual chatter two old friends make. I had been a consultant to Carolyn's company for several years, during which we discovered we shared many interests, and more importantly, developed a mutual trust. As any consultant will tell you, the time between the end of the main course and coffee is when the client gets down to the reason why you are both there, and this meal was no exception. After the coffee was poured, Carolyn leaned over the table and said in earnest, "We've *got* to do something. We've got to stop all of the grumbling—it's eating us alive."

Carolyn was the vice president of human resources for a large retail chain that was owned by an even larger and substantially more aggressive firm in the Northeast. The parent company had pushed, pulled, reorganized, and downsized its Western sibling many times over the past three years, with little noticeable improvement. Now, everyone was wringing their hands, and the pressure was on Carolyn to do something.

Joe, Carolyn's boss and the company president, was bitter. His attitude was: "These employees should be happy they still have jobs and if they're not, fire them. I'm not going to continue to coddle a bunch of whiners." As you might imagine, most of the employees were equally disgruntled, feeling that they had been jerked around one too many times. They would do the minimum required to keep their jobs, but no more. Even the most unobservant visitor to those offices of just under 10,000 people left with a sense of the anger and futility there. More than once I heard several people comment that maybe it would be better if they just closed the whole thing down.

"What are we going to do?" Carolyn asked. "Everyone seems to hate their job, including me. How can we turn this mess around?"

I was stumped. With a top boss who blamed the employees, and employees who, for the most part, blamed management, what could they do? They were caught in a downward spiral that only top management could stop.

Functioning in the System

The only way a company can eschew the culture of narcissism is to start at the top of the organization and push change downward. An attempt to try such a dramatic and serious change without the support and influence of top management is doomed to be an ultimate failure.

Sometimes organizational change isn't possible. When top management is ensconced in narcissistic practices, what do you do? Leave? Try to change the organization yourself? Most often, neither of those is a viable alternative. In these cases, you must learn to function within a narcissistic system without being destroyed by it. In this chapter we will examine strategies for working within a culture of narcissism without losing your ethics or your sanity.

Working successfully with a narcissistic manager is obviously not easy, but it can be done. Awareness of the narcissistic style and its origins is a good place to start in learning to work with the narcissist. In addition, there are some specific actions you can take to help neutralize the narcissistic environment and to maintain a healthy, productive working relationship.

KNOW YOURSELF

The first step in learning how to work with a narcissist begins by looking at yourself. The old adage "know yourself" has never been truer. Know myself? But isn't narcissism *his* problem? As strange as it may seem, the first step in being able to successfully work with a narcissist starts with a strong and comfortable knowledge of yourself. More specifically, you must examine your needs and your preferences for satisfying them. After all, half of your working relationship with a narcissist consists of how *you* respond.

When you fail to understand your own needs, you are unable to understand why you respond to the narcissist as you do. You can only know others at the depth with which you know yourself.

YOU CAN'T CHANGE THE NARCISSIST

Equally as important as knowing yourself is acknowledgment that you cannot change the narcissist. Nothing short of intensive therapy or significant self-discovery is going to change the long-standing personality of a narcissist. Once a narcissist has been successful enough to attain a management position, he has had years of reinforcement for narcissistic behaviors. Behaviors that root themselves in childhood, are intricately connected with his self-esteem, and have been used successfully for years are not changed quickly or easily. This kind of change takes a painful process of hard work over years to be successful. Ultimately, the narcissist must decide to change, and no one can make that decision for him.

Pointing out the need for change won't help; in fact, it will probably make things worse. After all, his narcissistic ways have served him well over the years, why should he stop now?

The real tragedy of the narcissist is that most seek help only after everything has fallen apart. The narcissistic cycle is so stubborn that usually only the threat of complete personal breakdown brings the impetus for change. That help often requires the long process of reframing an entire life. This is something only the narcissist can do for himself.

If you can't change the narcissist, then the only alternative is to accept him as he is. The success of the relationship depends heavily upon your ability to recognize his needs for what they are and to work within those limits. Until change does occur, any success in the relationship depends on how you respond.

WHAT ARE YOUR OWN NEEDS?

The motivations of the narcissist fall into two general categories: a strong need for power and a need for recognition. These two categories of needs overshadow everything he does. To discover how you can work with a narcissist, it is helpful to think of yourself in terms of these two classes of needs.

What needs are you trying to satisfy in this relationship? What motivates you? Take an assessment of your own needs for power and recognition and consider how you might be using your relationship with the narcissist to satisfy them. Since business relationships are very often the agents we use satisfy our needs, it is extremely important that you acknowledge what you need from the narcissist.

THE THREE "Cs"

You will find that most difficulties in your relationship with a narcissist occur because you are both determinably trying to satisfy the same needs, perhaps even with the same methods. The three most common difficulties that arise when this happens are:

1. *Competition*. Competition occurs when two people are trying to reach the same goal, one wins and the other must lose, and both must constantly gauge their performance against the other's to know their standing. Competition destroys cooperation, teamwork, and mutual assistance in a relationship.
2. *Conflict*. Like two countries fighting over the same land, conflict occurs when both parties are actively working to undermine, outsmart, and control the other in order to gain power. When territories overlap or have uncertain boundaries, disputes about who is in control and who answers to whom inevitably arise.
3. *Incompatibility*. Incompatibility occurs when one party is primarily focused on fulfilling internal motivations and the other is focused on extrinsic motivations. Their respective behaviors become an enigma to each other—a source of complete confusion. At the extreme, neither understands the reasons for the other's behaviors.

What follows is a closer look at each of these and some strategies for working through them when they occur. It is important to keep in mind that none of these will completely fix the situation, but they will help you keep your sanity *and* your job.

COMPETITION

When the need for recognition is active in both persons it can be a source of friction in a business relationship. When two people are trying to accomplish the same goal and receive credit for the accomplishment, competition is the outcome.

TRYING TO WORK AT THE SAME TASK

Take, for example, Margaret and Leonard, who work in the systems department of a large law firm. Both are trying to satisfy their need for recognition by accomplishing something that will grab the attention and recognition of the firm's senior partners. Margaret, department manager and Leonard's boss, presented a plan to implement a PC network and place a computer in every secretary's and attorney's office. She did an excellent job in the presentation to the firm's partners of showing just how easy the proposed system would make such mundane tasks as file sharing among attorneys, retrieving archived documents, editing existing documents, maintaining a calendar of appointments, and tracking billable hours. The partners were so impressed, they readily approved her proposal and encouraged her to speed up her implementation plan. Anxious to have a big win with the partners, Margaret began excitedly working on every aspect of the network implementation.

On the other hand, Leonard was new to the firm, eager to prove his skills, and well-trained and experienced in networks. He suddenly found that Margaret was involved in projects he felt he could handle better alone. Before long, Leonard began deliberately hiding many of the details of the project from Margaret for fear that she would get involved even further. Their conversations with each other about the project began taking an argumentative tone, as each was determined to prove they were right and the other was wrong. By the time the project was completed, it had gone considerably over the timeline and budget due to the amount of rework that had to be done. Because they had both been so intently involved in doing their own thing, a number of aspects of the system went unattended.

This example shows the competition that can arise between two people trying to "win" at the same task. Because they both were trying to satisfy their needs, they were driven to not only accomplish the project but to be personally recognized for it. Once the competition began, there had to be a winner and a loser and both were striving to be the winner.

Resolving the Problem

Below are four ways that a competitive situation like the one described could have been successfully resolved, with both Margaret and Leonard satisfying their needs for recognition:

1. Margaret could have made it clear which areas she would design and which Leonard would design. Also, she could have reassured Leonard that he would receive the credit for the areas he completed.

2. Leonard could have shown Margaret how the eventual success of his ideas would support the success of her broader objectives.

3. Margaret could have included Leonard in her presentations to the firm's partners.

4. If Margaret were unwilling to do any of the above, Leonard could have requested to take on an additional project in which he could personally excel.

What Margaret and Leonard should not do:

1. Neither should accept the idea that one must win and the other lose. While the temptation to fall into this thinking

is great, it is much more effective to define success cooperatively.

2. Margaret should not try to "teach Leonard a lesson" by sabotaging his efforts or passively allowing him fail. (As juvenile as this may sound, it is a very common tactic that overachieving managers use.)

Suggestions for Handling Competition

1. Create a clear division of labor. Both parties should know what tasks they are responsible for succeeding on with as little overlap between the two as possible.
2. Show the other party how your success will support them achieving their success. In other words, let the other person know that you are not interested in "stealing their thunder" but rather in helping them to make an even bigger noise.
3. Don't be greedy. When appropriate, share the spotlight with the other person. Let them receive the credit they deserve.
4. When all else fails, find another project that satisfies your need for recognition and achievement.

CONFLICT

Just as in the need for recognition, the need for power can cause difficulties in business relationships when it is high in both parties.

WORKERS AT ODDS

Consider the example of Tom, who is a human resources representative for a manufacturing division of a large high tech company. Tom often has to work with Jeff, who is the corporate director of compensation and benefits, on payroll issues for the managers he serves. Both Tom and Jeff have a high need for power and for feeling that they are in control of all the elements of their jobs. In meetings with the managers that he serves, Tom is often asked direct questions about promotions and salary increases. He likes to respond with a solid and definitive answer. Rather than always saying, "I'll get back to you on that," Tom prefers to give an answer on the spot, when possible.

Conflict often arises between Tom and Jeff because Jeff, who is responsible for the company's payroll budget, prefers to review and approve all salary increases before they are implemented. Because Jeff's predecessor allowed the human resources representatives to approve salary increases that fell within general guidelines, many of the representatives, including Tom, were resistant when Jeff retracted that freedom. Tom feels that this approval process really interferes with his ability to serve his managers, and on a number of occasions has gone ahead and implemented salary increases agreed upon by him and the managers with whom he works. Tom has earned an excellent reputation with his clients for cutting through the "red tape" and working with them to accomplish their business plans.

Jeff is furious that Tom is making decisions without his approval. Further, whenever Jeff calls Tom on the carpet for this, Tom marshals the support of his managers, making Jeff look like the bad guy. Over time, Tom and Jeff have found themselves at odds over almost every payroll change request Tom submits.

How to Avoid Conflict

To avoid escalating a conflict, Jeff and Tom could do the following:

1. Jeff and Tom could discuss the situation and come to an agreement on a clear division of responsibilities. For exam-

ple, Tom's role is to suggest appropriate salary adjustments, submit them to Jeff for approval, and facilitate a quick response. Jeff's role is to set the compensation policy and to keep Tom informed about any changes.

2. Tom could have discussed the project with Jeff on a higher, more strategic level, reaching agreement on the overall objectives but avoiding discussing the details. Once Jeff is involved in the details, his need for power will make it more difficult for him to back off. (This is similar to the strategy Jeff's predecessor used where he set the overall guideline and allowed the representatives approval authority within those guidelines.)

3. Tom could have agreed with Jeff's control over the larger project and requested to be given sole responsibility for some smaller piece. (e.g., Jeff sets the budget for increases in Tom's area and allows Tom discretion within those limits.)

4. Tom could have asked for additional responsibility for another project. (e.g., Tom could have asked for responsibility for the relocation and transfers program, providing another avenue for him to meet his power needs.)

Once the conflict has escalated, here are a few things Jeff and Tom should not do:

1. Jeff should not "lay down the law" and demand that Tom comply. This might be effective for the moment, but in the long run it will breed only more conflict and resentment. This tactic should only be used as a last resort.

2. Tom should not try to prove to Jeff that his way is wrong. Whether Jeff is right or wrong, once the need for power is roused, he is unlikely to back away from his stance.

3. Neither should exercise his formal or informal power to destroy the other. This can be effective in eliminating a rival, but it will invariably create more adversaries among those bystanders observing the conflict.

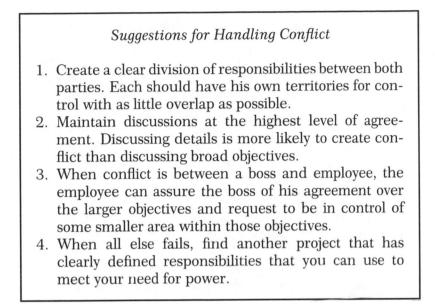

Suggestions for Handling Conflict

1. Create a clear division of responsibilities between both parties. Each should have his own territories for control with as little overlap as possible.
2. Maintain discussions at the highest level of agreement. Discussing details is more likely to create conflict than discussing broad objectives.
3. When conflict is between a boss and employee, the employee can assure the boss of his agreement over the larger objectives and request to be in control of some smaller area within those objectives.
4. When all else fails, find another project that has clearly defined responsibilities that you can use to meet your need for power.

COMPATIBILITY

One of the more robust measures of personality is the "locus of motivation." The locus of motivation has two possible outcomes: intrinsic or extrinsic. Generally speaking, persons with an intrinsic locus of motivation are energized by internal values and preferences. They do things because they like to do them or because they make them feel good. At the other extreme, persons with an extrinsic locus of motivation are prompted by external rewards and praise. The narcissist, as you might imagine, has an extrinsic loci of motivation.

Two people of extreme opposite loci of motivation, one of high extrinsic and the other high intrinsic, can often have compatibility difficulties. Compatibility refers to a person's ability to understand another's motivation—why they act the way they do. When two people are compatible they may not agree with each other, but they understand each other's motivations. On the other hand, two people who are incompatible find each other's behavior confusing and unpredictable. The key to the idea of compatibility is understanding another person's behavior.

A person who is of high extrinsic motivation tries to satisfy his needs by attaining external rewards. His behavior is guided by increases in salary, recognition, increased visibility, and other factors that can be seen by those around him. As a result, he is involved in activities that have a payout of external rewards. The person of high intrinsic motivation tries to satisfy his needs by doing what feels right, what is consistent with his values and helps him to increase his own competency. Consequently, he involves himself in activities that produce intrinsic consequences. As you might imagine, the kinds of things these two people find themselves doing are often quite different.

INCOMPATIBILITY AND DERAILMENT

For example, consider Julia and Leslie. Julia is a training specialist for a large retailer and Leslie, director of training, is her boss. Julia is highly intrinsically motivated and prefers to teach training programs that are consistent with her values. Committed to making the workplace a more enjoyable and harmonious experience, she prefers to hold training programs that deal with such things as relationships, team building, and empowerment. Julia also prefers to use custom training materials that deal with the issues of the specific group with which she is working. Because every group is different, they can rarely be prepared in advance. She sees little value in what she calls "canned" training materials.

Leslie, on the other hand, is highly extrinsically motivated and, as a result, prefers training programs that tackle more of the hard-core business issues and have a greater potential for bringing recognition from the executives of the company. She insists that all training programs have materials that are thoughtfully designed, professionally reproduced, and pleasing to the eye. She believes that a good trainer prepares a careful and interesting script that is followed each time that course is taught.

Leslie and Julia have difficulty understanding each other. Julia doesn't see the value of the programs that Leslie teaches and Leslie cannot understand why Julia wants to teach something that is secondary to business performance. When Julia teaches a program that Leslie has chosen, it inevitably takes on a "touchy-feely" twist and, of course, that drives Leslie crazy. Neither understands or values the contributions of the other.

Resolving the Differences

The greater the differences between two persons' loci of motivation, the tougher it is to resolve the differences. Steps that Julia and Leslie could have taken to lessen the differences might include the following:

1. Each could acknowledge that the other had a very different approach from their own and that both approaches could co-exist.

2. Leslie could have attempted to learn more about Julia's values and built a bridge by focusing on where their approaches are similar.

3. Julia could have chosen training programs that both provided intrinsic satisfaction for her and contributed to the business's bottom line, which would fulfill Leslie's extrinsic needs.

Suggestions for Handling Incompatibility

1. Understand that what motivates the other person is very different from what motivates you. Remind yourself that both approaches can co-exist.

2. Search each situation for what will motivate the other. When working with a narcissist, examine each working situation for what will meet his preference for extrinsic rewards and use that to motivate him in your direction.
3. Make decisions based on what will bring him extrinsic satisfaction and, at the same time, meet your intrinsic needs.

POINT OF NO RETURN

In the ideal world, every difficult work relationship could be resolved. But, in reality, it doesn't work that way. Sometimes, nothing works. This is when you've got to make the difficult decision to walk away.

A time may come when nothing can be done to salvage a working relationship with a narcissist. When threatened by an employee, he will eventually reach a point where he will cut off any chance of that employee succeeding and nothing, no matter how skillful or successful, will win back his support. He may even go so far as to set fatal traps for the disenfranchised employee, waiting for the first mistake. When this point is reached, it is time to leave. In this situation, leaving the department or the company is the only way to salvage a career and, more importantly, self-confidence. This can be a heart-rending decision and very difficult for those who are committed to their job, coworkers, and company. It is, however, a necessary decision and the only alternative. Staying may cost more than it is worth.

DEALING WITH YOUR ANGER

The second barrier you encounter may be your own anger. Undoubtedly the worst aspect of working for a narcissistic manager is all the anger that results from being exploited by him. Powerful rage often triggers knee-jerk reactions that aren't well thought out. That anger can fuel action that not only damages the career of the narcissist, but yours as well.

Dealing with the anger means acknowledging that you *are* angry. Unacknowledged anger can find many passive-aggressive means for expression. Talking about your feelings with someone who is outside work can help tremendously to diffuse the negative emotions.

Carefully consider how you discuss your feelings with fellow employees. The temptation to validate your feelings with those who may be experiencing the same is hard to resist, but you may find that such a discussion is not kept in the strictest of confidence and may only worsen your predicament. Especially try to avoid the temptation to strike back by broadcasting the error of the narcissist's ways; after all, not everyone may agree. In the long run, those tactics will reflect badly upon you. As always, those who sling the mud come out the dirtiest.

Equally as injurious is the anger you may have at yourself for allowing the manipulation. Anger directed inward is an insidious emotion that can undermine your self-confidence and your ability to do your job. Until you let yourself off the hook, you will never be able to detoxify your relationship with the narcissist. He will continue to arouse uncomfortable negative feelings that will prevent you from dealing with him in healthier and more productive ways.

RESISTANCE

Finally, a barrier that most encounter at some point in their attempts to work with a narcissist is *resistance*. Invariably when I work with a client on how to improve a relationship with a narcissist, they will say something like, "but you don't know so and so. Nothing I do will make a difference. He has to have complete control over everything!" In some cases, this is true. But more often than not, those despondent comments come from someone who is struggling to meet their own power or achievement needs. Often they have sacrificed much to needs of the narcissist and now find themselves unwilling to concede even in the slightest ways for the sake of compromise. In some situations, they can be even more dogmatic about imposing their wishes upon the relationship than the narcissist. The cumulative anger at having to serve someone else's needs when your own go wanting can create a heavy-handed determination to turn the tables in your favor and creates a strong resistance to considering anything that in some way accommodates the narcissist. Resistance can prevent you from seeing possible solutions and will eventually destroy an already faltering relationship.

Learning how to work with a narcissist requires patience, understanding, and an abundance of self-knowledge. Success at the relationship demands compromise and careful negotiation. To further complicate things, the anger, frustration, and resistance that the relationship provokes can serve to destroy it further if not carefully dealt with. Despite all this, it is possible to have a successful, productive relationship with a narcissist. Finding ways to satisfy your own needs that aren't in conflict with his can make the relationship a workable enterprise. Short of significant change, it is the only healthy way to work together.

NINE

A Second-Helping of Success

Despite the ubiquitous presence of narcissism in today's corporate environment, some companies do manage to stay out of the frenzied race toward self-interest. These companies are just as committed to growth and profit as any other; they simply envision another path to success. For them, success is not measured by the salary of a few executives and the dividends of distant shareholders; it is the gestalt of success upon the entire organization, employees and customers included. They strive to create an environment of openness and honesty that allows all to succeed who are willing to work hard and share their individual creativity.

ALMOST UTOPIA

Sound too utopian to be real? Well, maybe, but there are companies that are making significant headway toward these ideals, and one of the most impressive is Levi Strauss. This 140-year-old jeans maker out of San Francisco is breaking new ground and proving that profitability is not the exclusive right of those who leave their morals and humanity outside the corporate entrance.

Business at Levi, the world's largest apparel maker, has never been better. In 1995 the company had revenues of $6.7 billion and earned 11 percent of that figure in profits. Its newest line of cotton pants, Dockers, is proving that the company has its finger squarely on the pulse of the soft-in-the-middle, cash-rich baby boomers. Nearly seven in ten American men now own at least one pair of Dockers. Since the brand launched in 1986, this casual line has gone from nothing to a billion-dollar-plus business. To put this enormous success in perspective, Dockers would be a veritable Fortune 500 company if independent.

Robert Haas, CEO of Levi and the great-great-grand-nephew of the company founder, is proving that making money—and lots of it—isn't exclusive of strong social values. He has infused a strong sense of personal and corporate responsibility into a company that is often equated with the rugged individualism and free spirit of America's old West. Says Haas, "Companies have to wake up to the fact that they are more than a product on a shelf. They're behavior as well."[1]

Levi's commitment to values extends into all areas of the business, including the controversial overseas "sweat-shops" where much of America's apparel is manufactured. Today, more than half of Levi's products are manufactured overseas. So, nearly three years ago, the company instituted a set of ethical standards for doing business with foreign contractors. The resulting "Terms of Engagement" cover such areas as environmental, safety, and health requirements, even the right of free association. Once implemented, the company soon audited more than 600 of its overseas contractors and dismissed thirty of them for failure to meet the new guidelines.

In 1993, when China's most-favored-nation trading status was in question because of human rights violations, Levi voluntarily withdrew $40 million of business from the country. The company claimed the move wasn't political, but was rather a visible act putting freedom above profits.

Levi's work in Bangladesh in helping to attack child labor in the garment industry there is considered a model program. In 1994, the company discovered a Bangladeshi contractor employing children under the age of fourteen, the age set as the minimum for contract workers.

Levi executives faced a sticky dilemma: If the kids were fired, they'd be forced to work in another factory or, worse, panhandle in the streets. After some weighty considerations, Levi decided to open a school for the children at that contractor, pay them what they would have earned if they were working and, when they turned fourteen, offer them jobs in the factory.

"You can develop a set of guidelines you feel reflects your corporate values and aspirations. Then, in practice, you get new information and you're confronted with new situations like in Bangladesh," says Levi's public policy manager, Michael Kabuki. "We responded in a way that took us out of the four walls of the factory. We were able to look a little broader as to how these girls might be affected if they weren't working anymore."[2]

Levi's ethical approach to overseas operations was, at the time, in sharp contrast to other retailers. Most notably, in 1992 David Glass, chief executive officer of Wal-Mart, appeared on national television and questioned the validity of photographs depicting Bangladeshi children sewing shirts for the discount giant.

"The pictures you showed me mean nothing to me," Glass said to NBC's *Dateline* television program. Glass's attempt to deflect the situation backfired and resulted in a wave of negative publicity for the discount retailer. Only then did it take action to correct the problem in Bangladesh.[3]

Levi's ethics are much more than just a trendy nineties publicity campaign. Back home in the brick headquarters looking out over San Francisco Bay and the Golden Gate Bridge, Levi's commitment to values is serious business. The company has adopted an "Aspiration Statement" that is used to guide all company decisions:

WHAT LEVI'S ASPIRES TO

New Behaviors
Management must exemplify "directness, openness to influence, commitment to the success of others, and willingness to acknowledge our own contributions to problems."

Diversity
Levi's "values a diverse workforce (age, sex, ethnic group, etc.) at all levels of the organization. . . . Differing points of view will be sought; diversity will be valued and honestly rewarded, not suppressed."

Recognition
Levi's will "provide greater recognition—both financial and psychic—for individuals and teams that contribute to our success . . . those who create and innovate and those who continually support day-to-day business requirements."

Ethical Management Practices
Management should epitomize "the stated standards of ethical behavior. We must provide clarity about our expectations and must enforce these standards throughout the corporation."

Communications
Management must be "clear about company, unit, and individual goals and performance. People must know what is expected of them and receive timely, and honest feedback . . ."

Empowerment
Management must "increase the authority and responsibility of those closest to our products and customers. By actively pushing the responsibility, trust, and recognition into the organization, we can harness and release the capabilities of all our people."

The aspirations statement is printed on blue recycled paper made from old denim and is posted in all locations around the world and given to every new employee. One-third of an employee's performance evaluation is based on the fulfillment of aspirational behaviors. Ignore these values and you may not get a raise, or, worse, you may find yourself out of a job.[4]

As one might expect, Levi's commitment to socially responsible business hasn't been implemented with everyone's blessing. F. Warren Hellman, Haas's distant cousin and Levi board member, has criticized Levi's nontraditional management. "There's danger that this will degrade into a touchy-feely, I-don't-want-to-offend-you, creativity-stifling style of management."

But there is little reason to give credence to such stereotypic criticisms rooted in the assumptions of traditional corporate narcissism (i.e., business can't be successful unless it is highly competitive, hard-edged, and ruthless). Given Levi's unprecedented financial success, even Hellman admitted, "Basically, we love Bob. Bob has made a fortune for everyone . . ."[5]

Not So Rapid-Response

Levi's values-centered management style has survived trial by fire and proved its worth. In the early 1990s the company suffered a slowdown in sales and mounting complaints that customer service was dismal. Some customers were complaining that orders placed at the beginning of a season weren't being filled until the season was over, a fatal error in apparel retailing.

To fix the problem, Levi elicited advice from 6,000 of the company's 36,000 employees on what could be done to fix the problem. With that in hand, nearly 200 of the company's executives took over an entire floor at headquarters and spent a year (and $12 million) planning what should be changed. The company's Diversity Council, which represents various groups of employees, including blacks, Asians, Hispanics, gays, and women, played a role in the reengineering decisions.

After all the planning, Levi spent $400 million converting all thirty-seven of its North American factories to team manufacturing. The team approach replaced the more traditional assembly-line process where one worker repeats the same task over and over again. Each team is self-directed and produces garments from beginning to end. In addition, Levi trained plant employees in everything from conflict resolution to managing production flows.

And the collaborative approach is working. Tommye Jo Davis, manger of Levi's Murphy, North Carolina, plant, reports that defects dropped from more than 4 percent to around 2 percent after the team system was up and running. Most notably, the company has reduced the time it takes to replenish store shelves from three weeks to just shy of seventy-two hours.[6]

Honesty Is the Key

Robert D. Rocky, president of Levi Strauss North America, says that "honesty is key" to Levi's philosophy of management. To this point, the company has embraced the sometimes rocky process of 360° performance reviews. In this process a manager's performance is evaluated by not only the supervisor but peers and subordinates. Rocky says his own review "upset my self-image" and pushed him to command others less and listen more.

A recent hire from a New York investment firm reports putting the claims to openness and honesty to test shortly after joining Levi. After what she considered some heavy-handed behavior from her boss, she took a risk and privately called him on the carpet. To her surprise, the boss listened and agreed to change. "I found that Aspirations isn't about New Age feel-good. It's about being open and direct," she says.

Spreading the Wealth

In June 1996, Levi announced its most aggressive departure from the culture of corporate narcissism to date. Robert Haas announced what benefits specialists say may be the richest and most unusual employee reward program ever: If Levi reaches cumulative cash flow of $7.6 billion for the next six years, each of the company's 37,500 employees in sixty countries, regardless of position, will get a full year's pay as bonus. Called the Global Success Sharing Plan, it diverts 10 percent of the cash that would normally go to shareholders and returns it to employees. "Motivated employees are our source of innovation and competitive advantage," said Haas. "By acknowledging and rewarding their efforts we not only demonstrate our appreciation, but also encourage them to continue striving for new standards of excellence."[7]

Traditional business media, shocked by the breadth of the program, reported that it could "cost" shareholders of the company $750 million. While this is true, most reports failed to mention it will also earn those same investors a healthy return somewhere in the neighborhood of $7 billion. *Business Week* damned the program with faint praise, calling it admirable but questionable.[8]

SKEPTICAL MEDIA

The handling of Levi Strauss by the traditional business media is a window into the narcissistic attitudes that prevail in many areas of the corporate world. Aside from narrowly defined trade magazines, most corporate citizens rely on the news and advice of a relatively small number of business publications. These include *The Wall Street Journal*, *Fortune*, *Business Week*, and *Forbes*. Given the ever increasing demands of corporate life, these publications give many readers their only look inside other companies as well as assessments of more universal markets. What they publish and the context in which they place it carries tremendous power in shaping American business. Unfortunately, most are fully entrenched in narcissistic philosophies of business and allow that to seep into their reports of business news.

Take, for example, the manner in which *Business Week* has handled Levi Strauss. In 1994, the award-winning magazine ran a cover story titled "Managing By Values: Is Levi Strauss' Approach Visionary—Or Flaky?" and sarcastically opens with the words, "Talk, talk, talk." While the article does recount the unprecedented success of the company, more than half the article is given to pessimistic speculation about the company's future and quotes from Levi detractors.

One rather sophomoric quote comes from "noted" apparel consultant Alan G. Millstein, who said, "The Haases think they talk to God." Another quote, which was later referenced in a 1996 article,[9] associates the company with New Age "crystals," despite the fact the company has no connection to any New Age spiritualism. Clearly trying to associate the company with the anti-liberal political tone of the year, the article refers to Levi's management strategy as "traditional liberal idealism."

The nod to narcissism is most evident in the writer's attempt to show that Levi's success with values management is costly and idiosyncratic. "The simple truth is, living up to a value system as comprehensive as Levi's is hard. It takes hours and hours of work." The article concludes, "Dealing with the surprising, often contradictory results of managing by values may be a manager's toughest task. Many managers are likely to ask themselves: Is it worth the trouble? Many, perhaps, would say 'no.' " Thus, in one gallant swipe of the pen, *Business Week* absolves the remainder of the corporate world.

There isn't one shred of evidence to suggest that the management by values practiced at Levi is any more costly or time consuming than management at other firms. In fact, a strong case can be made that the internal competition and political maneuvering that is standard in many other organizations is far more costly. And that doesn't even begin to describe the difference in quality of life Levi managers enjoy.

Levi shows all the elements of shunning a culture of narcissism: honesty in dealing with employees and customers, extensive training, clear and revered values, and peer and subordinate performance reviews. These and other techniques help the organization maintain its momentum. Arguably, many of these factors are directly linked to the company's continuous financial success.

IT WORKS IN SMALL COMPANIES, TOO

But what about smaller, younger companies that must deal with turbulent markets and international competition. Can they afford to pursue the same path as Levi? If the case of Pro Fasteners, Inc. in San Jose, California, is any indication, they can't afford not to.

LOW TECH BUT HIGH MARKS

Pro Fasteners Inc (PFI) is about as low tech as a company operating in Silicon Valley can be. They don't make computer chips, supercomputers, fiber optic communications, or some other science-fiction-come-to-life product. Simply, they are the equivalent of a very large industrial hardware store to the companies that do make the high tech components and gadgets that have made Silicon Valley world renown. PFI supplies all of the ordinary nuts-and-bolts used in the manufacturing of electronic equipment.

PFI is run by its founder, Steve Braccini, an engaging and warm forty-something man who is, by his own admission, something of a Type A personality. Braccini runs a company that has grown and succeeded through ten years of wild fluctuations in the economic fortunes of high tech companies. More importantly, he has created a company where teams thrive and narcissism has no place.

The insight and inspiration that created the open and empowered culture at PFI is inextricably linked to Braccini's personal transformation. During the early years of business, Braccini structured the company like most, with himself on the top looking down, shielded by a thick layer of middle management, and employees on the bottom, bearing the weight and brunt of company. He ran the business by his sheer force of will. In the office early, he'd spend his days working the phones, giving orders, and making sure he had a finger in every company pie. Evenings after work, he'd retire with a bottle.

But it was in 1990 that Braccini's transformation began with a stay at the Betty Ford Clinic. The twenty-eight-day stay at the clinic was one that revolutionized his life. For one thing, he began to discover the "self" that had long hidden under cloak of alcohol and overwork. Many of the hard-earned insights into himself also began to relate to PFI. As Braccini now puts it, "I began to realize a lot of things about myself and the theories I had about myself for some reason corresponded to the business. The better I took care of my-self, for example, the better I felt and the better I did. It was like this light went on. 'Oh—so the better I take care of the customers, the better they'll feel about me . . .' And it just went on from there."

Braccini's return to sobriety was the beginning of a re-markable change for PFI. In a nutshell, he returned deter-mined to "turn the pyramid upside down" and allow the employees—the people on the front lines of the busi-ness—to have a say in problem solving and managing the organization. The changes he imposed on PFI sent tremors through every department and every job. Not everyone liked his ideas and, as a result, not everyone—including his wife—stayed on with the company.

Several years later, PFI can boast of a continuous-im-provement quality program that resulted in near-perfect cus-tomer service. The company sports a million-dollar, state-of-the-art computer system that offers services that are virtually unheard of in its industry. Internally, the company is run, in large part, by cross-functional teams that involve employees at every level. Best and most impressive of all, PFI is growing and prospering in an industry that considers 3 percent a healthy net profit.

How did Braccini pull off this remarkable transformation? It wasn't easy, and there were a few casualities along the way. He started by announcing that the ultimate responsibility for the business's operation would lie with each employee. Day-to-day managerial responsibility would rest on the shoulders of the line managers and he, the hands-on CEO, would pull back, empowering his managers and concentrating instead on strategic planning.

Braccini created a powerful internal body called the Continuous Improvement Council (CIC) to which he gave responsibility for creating and managing teams in all areas of the business. The CIC has the authority to do anything that is necessary to improve quality and customer service. Its mandate covers all areas of managerial and departmental control.

The list of CIC and team accomplishments is long and varied. One team figured out how to alter the order-processing system to eliminate early shipments, which were responsible for about 5 percent of all rejects from customers. Another group streamlined warehouse procedures so the company could ship by 4 p.m. all orders received before noon. Still another worked specifically with Applied Materials, one of PFI's primary customers, to ensure 100 percent on-time delivery of 100 percent correct parts.

Braccini's shift in focus also increased his own productivity. He began to plan for the business he envisioned—a supplier that was integrated into the customer's business. No longer would PFI simply wait for the customer to run out of a part and then call to place an order. Braccini wanted a PFI that could keep the part on the customer's shelf and continuously in stock. His vision was of a company that was actually integrated—at times even located—within the customer's place of business.

That's where the million-dollar computer came into

being. By locating a terminal at the customer's location, PFI could monitor parts inventory and manage it for its customers. The computer would automatically generate orders, invoices, and buy lists for Pro's purchasing department. Warehouse workers would carry portable bar-code scanners that would give instant inventory information to PFI and, hence, the customer. In time, Braccini was able to make this vision a reality, offering to his customers better service than any of his competitors could even imagine.

All of these cross-functional, organization-wide changes meant that managers could no longer maintain strict control over their departments. They could influence, support, and even problem-solve issues relating to their departments, but they could no longer strong-arm processes that spanned over many managers and departments. Employees at all levels were empowered to speak and, more importantly, to be heard. It is no wonder that some managers who preferred the more traditional methods of control and delegation couldn't function within the new PFI.

The most notable loss was of Steve's wife, Cinde Braccini, who had managed many of the day-to-day operations of the company since it began. She thought the idea of allowing employees to have such influence over the company was crazy. She remembers, "I'd walk in on certain days and say, 'Well, is it bad enough now? Can we stop?' " To her, it was like "the inmates' running the asylum." Eventually, she along with other managers, including the company controller, found the changes too much, and they left the company. (Yes, it was a strain on the Braccini's marriage, but they proudly admit they have been able to get over it.)

Those who stayed learned the value of open and honest communication. The newly hired general manager, Robert Landau, found out just what that means within the first few months of working at PFI. Several employees got together and confronted Landau about being "too cold and blunt." Much to Landau's surprise, what first looked like a lynch mob became a productive and civil feedback session. Landau took the advice and softened his style, learning to be more of a coach than an umpire. One worker who was part of that early confrontation now says "Robert has totally blossomed."

It is of no small significance that a warehouse employee feels he has the right to address the management style of the general manager (or any other management issue, for that matter). In many organizations, such a move would be considered career suicide. At PFI it is considered continuously improving the business.

At the time of this writing, PFI has continued to grow in double digits. Each year brings double and triple industry average profits. The road continues to be rocky, but PFI is as committed as ever to maintaining an open, honest, and continually improving culture. Braccini sums up the process well: "We've been learning to walk, then trot, and then run fast. Now we're ready to compete."[10]

REFUSING TO SUCCUMB

The companies who have refused to succumb to the seductive culture of narcissism are many, although their stories aren't often publicized. David Bollier, in a book titled *Aiming Higher*,[11] writes the stories of twenty-five different companies that have followed a socially responsible path and, not inconsequentially, attained a good measure of financial success.

PEOPLE MAKE THE DIFFERENCE

One of those stories is of Starbucks Coffee Company. After only ten years of operation, the company has grown phenomenally despite the fact that the nation's coffee consumption has decreased by a third in recent years. By the end of fiscal 1995, Starbucks boasted of 676 coffee bars nationwide and has enjoyed an 80–100 percent growth in revenue every year of its existence. 1995 revenues topped out at $465 million.

Starbucks chairman, Howard Schultz, sums up the company's formula for success: "If I am asked as chairman of the company, what is the single reason why Starbucks has been able to achieve its objective qualitatively and quantitatively, I always recite . . . that our people are making the difference."

Schultz decided early in the company's history to offer a generous and comprehensive benefits package to both part-time and full-time employees. The package includes stock options, health care, training programs, career counseling, and product discounts. To Schultz, part-time workers were more than just interchangeable counter help; they were the lifeblood of the company. The cost of turnover and employee training far outweighed the cost of the benefits.

In the beginning, not everyone—including a few members of Starbucks's board of directors—approved of Schultz's generosity. Again Schultz describes: "I would ask the cynics, how could you afford not to do this? We have lowered our attrition rate to such a low level that it's a glaring advantage in terms of retail workers . . . The financial performance of the company, given the growth rate, is probably second to none of any retailer in America today."

Starbucks' commitment to its employees is essential to maintaining and delivering high product quality. Every new employee spends about twenty-four hours in training learning all the details of the business, including the history of coffee and how to prepare the perfect cup.

REAPING THE REWARD

Companies like Levi Strauss, Pro Fasteners, Inc., and Starbucks exemplify the fact that financial success does not come only at the expense of employees and customers. By insisting on values that make the corporation a truly social entity, the owner/shareholders have reaped the reward that comes from an organization that has added real value to the marketplace.

Looking at Ourselves

As you've read this far through this book, do you see a bit of yourself in the narcissist? If you do, then you're like most people. Those who have spent any time within the corporate arena have found themselves engaging in the tactics of the narcissist. The truth is, narcissistic potential resides within each of us. How we deal with our own need for approval, power, and success determines how we manage in the corporation. Growing beyond the tactics of the narcissist and learning to find career success through healthier methods is not only personally fulfilling, it is far more productive for the organization.

Take a minute to read the following questions. How many of these apply to you?

☐ Do you see people as falling into two categories—winners and losers?
☐ Do you worry that your share isn't large enough and your credit too small?
☐ Do you get upset if others fail to acknowledge your position in the corporate hierarchy or get your title wrong?
☐ Do you overuse and even abuse your management strengths? (For example, Do you use your knowledge of the industry to show off, dominate, or humiliate others?)
☐ When you encounter difficulties at work, do you blame ex-

ternals—bad luck, the economy, the ineptitude of other
people to explain your failures?
☐ Do you dwell on critical remarks, imagining how you might
avoid or downplay them?
☐ Does your anger boil into rage over trivial events?
☐ Do you spend more time thinking about how to outsmart
other associates and departments in the company than the
competition or meeting the customer's needs?
☐ Do you see yourself spending more time and energy on
work and less with family and friends than most people?

All of these questions point to certain narcissistic tendencies. They point to issues which, out of control, become serious problems within the organization. By making ourselves
aware of our own behavior, we move one step closer to eliminating narcissism from the organization.

In the following sections, I have listed several faulty "life
assumptions" which underlie the narcissistic condition. As
you read through them, think about your own assumptions
and challenge yourself when you find a difference.

"My Worth Is Based On My Position, Rank Or Salary, Not on Who I Am."

"I am somebody special because others acknowledge my
excellence." "I can be proud because I have been able to attain goals others have only dreamed of." "Because I have done
good things, I am good."

Doesn't sound all that bad, does it? Well consider the
other half of what hasn't been said: "I am nobody if others do
not see me as great." "I have no right to be proud because I
do ordinary things." "I am a bad person when I do bad things."

The real danger in this belief is at the extremes—where
the narcissist lives. The narcissist uses natural logic to figure
"if I want to be worthwhile, then I must appear as worthwhile." When you think this way, you will find yourself frequently about the business of proving your self-worth to
others, rather than doing something that might make a difference for yourself and others. In the narcissistic extreme, you

spend most of your time inventing ways to prove your worth to other people.

You are worthwhile because you are you. Cliché, cliché, cliché, but true. You are valuable because of your uniqueness, and the best you can do in life is to reach inside yourself and share that uniqueness with your family, friends, and your job. That is your only real value. There is nothing you can do to increase your personal worth. Nothing.

"Bad Feelings Should Be Avoided At All Cost."

Nobody likes a sad story and a long face, but the truth is, life is filled with both the happy and the sad. When you repress the sad and sweep it under a counterfeit smile, you equally lessen the intensity of your happiness. It is only by knowing sorrow that joy has any meaning. When you learn that some feelings are not acceptable, you deny their expression and push them down in your consciousness. Eventually, you lose the capacity to feel much of anything.

The narcissist allows himself to feel only acceptable feelings and thereby kills all but the most irrepressible emotions. He then must manufacture the appropriate public response to emotional situations. He appears sad when close associates leave the firm. He responds with delight when others are promoted. He may even conjure up a good facsimile of righteous indignation when he uncovers the unseemly tactics of a corporate foe.

By killing off emotion, the narcissist drains life of its texture and flavor. He has reduced his existence to a bland menu of the appropriate. Consequently, he is always searching for the one more success or award that will give him satisfaction. Life becomes something of a joyless treadmill.

"Never Admit Mistakes."

Admitting to failure is a sign of weakness. Linked to the idea that your worth is connected to what you accomplish, failure signifies that your self-worth is somehow less. You are less of a person when you fail and, consequently, to confess your vulnerability is to devalue yourself.

The narcissist will most certainly not admit a mistake or weakness. The lean-to of his invented self is too weak to withstand such an attack. He must explain away what appear to be his mistakes or weaknesses as someone else's responsibility. A good example of this is when he is asked that ridiculous interview question, "What would you say is your biggest weakness?" Predictably, he will pause thoughtfully and reply with a well-phrased false negative like "I work too much" or "I am too conscientious" rather than admitting to a true weakness. As painful as it is, the road to change demands that you be willing to own *who you are,* both strengths and weaknesses.

The truth is that it often takes more courage to admit failure than to accept the credit for success. Mistakes are rich with information and learning. Without them, we never discover the parameters of success. As the eminent psychologist George Kelly once noted, the world has benefited more from Christopher Columbus's mistake than from almost any other intentional victories.

Acknowledging a mistake and learning from it prevents one from repeating the error. If we leave mistakes buried and unexamined, we are doomed to repeat them. Not only is this unproductive; it is ultimately the definition of insanity: the continual repetition of ineffectual behaviors.

"Focus On The Future Instead of the Present."

The best escape from experiencing today in all of its raw depth is to spend your time thinking about how tomorrow will be better. A never-ending chase of tomorrow creates a sort of psychological salve that allows us to endure today's pain. You may think, Tomorrow your ship will come into port and all will be better. But for the narcissist, that day never comes. If it did, he would be forced to come to grips with himself and the pain he has worked so hard to suppress. Keeping a steady focus on the future is a primary tool the narcissist uses to deny his pain and to avoid experiencing his true self.

Living in the present requires an openness toward reality.

One must be willing to accept what the moment offers and to experience that moment without trying to fix it first. If anything, good business decisions demand that one strip away the fantasies and denials and see the situation for what it is. By living in the future, we cloud our judgment with fantasies of what we wish today would become. More than one enterprise has faltered because a narcissistic leader based critical business decisions on his grandiose fantasies of the future rather than on the cold reality of the present.

"No One Does It as Good as I Do It."

Because the narcissist works to prove his self-worth, he needs to see things done his way. Consequently, he will personally take on the responsibility for any number of projects and insist that they be done according to his instruction. To see a project done according to someone else's idea would have no impact on his self-worth and would undermine his motivations.

No two people work exactly alike. Fortunately, there are endless roads to success, and there is opportunity for each person to take the route of her own choosing. By insisting that others do things exactly as you would do them, you diminish the ultimate outcome. Because others are not you, their efforts will only approximate but never equal your own. To insist that others limit themselves to imitating you is to settle for less than what they might otherwise produce.

"The Value Of Other People Is Based On What They Can Do For Me."

Other people are the vehicle the narcissist uses to carry out his objectives. Because he finds it difficult to identify and understand the feelings of others, he often treats them as merely objects to be manipulated. Particularly in business, his relationships play a big role in confirming his self-worth by helping him to achieve. When others are of no further use, he will often abandon the relationship.

This attitude toward others creates ill will throughout the

organization. Nobody wants to feel as if they have been only used for another's gain. The resulting disillusionment creates a demoralized staff and severely damages company loyalty.

"Only Tasks Of High Visibility Are Worthwhile."

Since the narcissist's primary purpose is to achieve recognition and praise for his conquests, it only makes sense that he would selectively pick the projects that have the greatest potential. Doing something because it is the right thing to do or because it needs to be done isn't enough reason to propel him to action. This is especially true if few people will acknowledge the effort. The narcissist sees little to be gained from that type of situation.

"I Must Always Appear to Be in Control."

The narcissist cringes at the thought of appearing out of control. After all, that is what he assumes he is paid to do: control those who are under him. If others are left to their own devices, the result will surely be disastrous. He must never appear to be out of control, because his people might take advantage of such a weakness.

This is nothing more than the narcissist's projection of his own need for power. He assumes others are equally motivated to control him. Control or be controlled. He must counteract those other forces by being the first to take control.

"I Must Be Involved In Every Decision Below Me."

The narcissistic manager will involve himself in any decision, both important and trivial. Everything from million-dollar budget decisions to the purchase of office supplies presents an opportunity for him to impose his ideas on his surroundings. By involving himself in decisions at all levels, he can be assured that his ideas are being implemented.

"I Must Surround Myself With People Who Share My Point Of View."

Call it building a team, creating a common vision and values, or just plain old cronyism, the narcissistic manager will surround himself with individuals who, at a minimum, are unwilling to voice a dissenting opinion, and, at best, are willing to support his programs and ideas without question. He knows that having to convince someone on his staff that he is right and they are wrong can interfere with the successful implementation of his agenda and present a challenge to his control of the department. Dissension in the ranks slows his achievements and diminishes his appearance of control.

SOFTENING THE NARCISSISTIC MANAGEMENT STYLE

If you find that you need additional help changing your own management style, there are several readily available sources. Three of the more common are:

1. Executive coaches
2. 360° surveys
3. Management seminars

Executive Coaches

One of the best and most effective methods for working with a narcissist is the executive coach. Like a sort of management therapist, the executive coach can effectively mirror back to the manager his own behavior and help him understand some of the implications of that behavior. The coach can consult on specific work projects and relationships and help the manager see specifically the impact of his management style and how he might do things differently. In order for the executive coach to be successful, however, the manager must be willing to acknowledge that he, not his boss, not his staff, and not the company, has a problem that needs help. It is not uncommon for a manager to hire executive coaches to garner expert opinion about the problems of everyone around him, excluding himself. Such political maneuvering is a waste of both the coach's and manager's time and is, of course, completely ineffective in changing behavior.

The typical arrangement with an executive coach begins

with anywhere from a half-day to several half-day meetings. During these initial meetings the coach may use a variety of instruments and exercises to collect data on the manager's self-perceptions as well as the perceptions of those who work with the manager. The coach will want to collect a fair amount of biographical history from the manager and talk about the manager's relationships both inside and outside of work. Following the initial meetings, the manager and coach will usually meet once a week for anywhere from three to six months, or longer if necessary. During these meetings, the manager and coach will talk about the events of the past week, how the manager handled them, and any "homework" assignments the two had agreed on in previous meetings. These meetings are usually held after hours at the manager's place of work or outside of work to ensure privacy and confidentiality. The work between the coach and the manager is strictly confidential and should never be reported in any form to higher management.

Surveys

Surveys, when properly used and interpreted, can be a powerful tool to be used in giving honest feedback to a narcissistic manager. The most commonly used is the 360° survey, a survey that collects data from the full circle of those around the manager—the boss, co-workers, subordinates, the manager and sometimes, customers. The items on the survey can cover any number of issues, but generally center on the manager's management style. Powerful comparisons can be drawn between the manager's perceptions of his behavior and others' perceptions. This tool helps jump-start the narcissistic manager's vicarious learning cycle.

Warning! Surveys should be used with the utmost care and administered by a trained professional. It is not uncommon at all for a mishandled and misinterpreted survey to fall into the hands of a manager who uses it as ammunition against his enemies. The survey should be administered with very clear and strict guidelines and personally interpreted by a trained professional. A solid survey program includes several follow-up meetings with the professional and a specific survey action plan.

Seminars

Although seminars are the most accessible of these tools, they are the least effective at bringing about behavioral change. It is simply too difficult in a classroom of twenty or more other managers to deal with the specific issues of each manager. Seminars are most useful as a tool for raising awareness to a problem or technique and introducing the student to the sources that provide ongoing support for change. The seminar itself can never provide all the impetus and support needed for large-scale change. While the seminar is useful, it should not be viewed as a panacea for changing the narcissistic manager.

Awareness of your own narcissistic tendencies is the very first step in eliminating those practices from the organization at large. By becoming aware and refusing to enable the narcissism of others, you can make a marked difference. Awareness is the first step toward an organization where success is defined collectively. This is the beginning of a more enlightened self-interest.

Epilogue
Reversing the Flow

During the closing months of 1995, fire raced through a relatively small textile mill in Lawrence, Massachusetts, destroying all but one of the company's buildings. As tragic as this fire was for Malden Mills' owners and workers, it was hardly the stuff of national news. That is, not until the president of the company, Aaron Feuerstein, did something that much of the business community considered extraordinary: He continued to pay employees while the charred mill was rebuilt.

Every major newspaper and network carried the story. Even the venerable news programs *Nightline* and *60 Minutes* rushed to the textile mill town of Lawrence to record the remarkable executive who was risking his personal fortune to care for his employees. President Clinton even summoned him to the White House to honor his heroic deed. Since then, he has been showered with honorary degrees.

Feuerstein's loyalty to his employees is in stark contrast to Lawrence's other claim to history: the Bread and Roses labor strike of 1912. That labor strike was ignited by mill owner William Wood, who came to symbolize the slave-driving, profit-mongering arrogance of the mill owners at the time. Only after a bitter struggle the workers won a shortened work week (from seven to six days a week), a pay raise, and basic improvements in safety and working conditions.

Feuerstein is cut from a different cloth. No less of a businessman, he practices a different brand of management. In his words, "the people will make or break the quality of the product. They stand there on the line, making the cloth, examining the cloth and they make it superior to the competition. So I don't think it's illogical to say that the loyalty extended to people brings back loyalty from them, which makes the difference."

The story of Feuerstein and Malden Mills is in vivid contrast to the nihilistic, self-serving world of corporate narcissism. As in the labor oppressed days of 1912, narcissistic managers try to take as much as they can and give back the least amount possible. But that's not the philosophy of Feuerstein, nor can it be of any other manager who wants to attain a collective, corporate success.

THE PRINCIPLE OF LAGNIAPPE

The seventy-year-old Feuerstein discovered a basic management principle that few of today's "experts" know. No one sustains a profit from giving less. No company grows from constant cutting. The "pruning" gardening analogy and "lean-and-mean" sports analogy so popular with corporate reengineering gurus are misplaced comparisons—excuses for taking the easy path to quick payouts.

But these chilling voices are wrong. Their words are leading not a few companies down a trail of demoralized and de-intellectualized ruination. Corporate America will not prosper under another decade of continuous, traumatic trimming and a focus on profit at any price. This narcissistic crusade flies in the face of the most basic principle of human behavior. It is the principle of *lagniappe* (pronounced *lan-yap'*).

It wasn't psychologists who first discovered this lesson in human behavior; rather, it was the French businessmen in New Orleans during the 18th century. These barons of commerce learned the value of balancing the social equation and created the word *lagniappe* to label their discovery. At first, lagniappe referred to a little bit extra that was thrown in after a deal was made. It wasn't required or expected, it was simply a gift—a little more—that was thrown in for good measure. In time, the word acquired a more general meaning, referring to any thing or any action that was given above the call of duty.

Why did they practice lagniappe? Were these business-men simply overly generous? Were they prone to giving away more of their product or service than was necessary? Perhaps it was nothing more than a bribe. None of these was true. Those colonial businessmen understood in real terms the power of the social equation: when they gave a little more, they got a little more. When they gave more than what was merely required, it was like saying, "the value of our relation-ship goes beyond this present deal." Maybe not at the mo-ment, but sometime in the future, that customer would be back with more business. These French businessmen learned a powerful psychological principle: When you give lagniappe, others feel valued and are motivated to return lagniappe.

This is nothing more than what psychologists call social equity: the ratio of one's inputs and outputs in a relationship. In a corporate culture of narcissism, that equation is grossly out of balance. Employees in these organizations have watched while their paychecks shrink with inflation and cor-porate executives receive enormous raises and even bigger bo-nuses. The pay gap has widened so much that it isn't unusual for senior executives to make over 100 times what the average, college-educated, new employee makes. And as dramatic as this is, the inequality is about much more than just money. As a result of downsizing, the majority of U.S. workers are report-ing continually increasing workloads. Job stress is at an all-time high, and employee morale and satisfaction are at record lows.

The imbalance between what the senior executive re-ceives and what the average worker receives is clearly evident. The resulting frustration is in no small part what fueled the extremist policies of Pat Buchanan's presidential bid in 1996. The leaders of the Grand Old Party were visibly shocked not only by Buchanan's criticisms of corporate actions, but by the amount of support those criticisms yielded among party mem-bers.

Despite the fact that many companies are giving much less, lagniappe is what these companies want from their employees. They have cut everything from employee benefits to pay raises and promotions, and, at the same time, beg for more creativity and attention to quality. This forced equation will never balance with the current narcissistic values. The culture of narcissism inevitably destroys the practice of the lagniappe principle.

Lagniappe is essential to innovation and, therefore, to business growth. By the definition of the word, innovation is something extra—something previously undiscovered that employees give to the company. It can't be required, demanded, or written into a contract. True innovation can only be offered from a mind that is willing to give. The company that practices lagniappe opens the door for new ideas, new products, and new markets.

Companies exist that do practice the lagniappe principle. Do these companies pay their employees more than those who don't? Do these enlightened workplaces practice a soft, expensive, paternalistic form of "family employment?" Are these the dreamy corporate campuses skirted with landscaped lawns where casually dressed employees come and go at self-determined hours? Not always.

The practice of lagniappe is *not* the old philosophy of paying higher salaries to get more and better work. Companies that use it have discovered that the power of lagniappe lies not in giving more money, but in selectively giving more of what is important and meaningful to the recipient. They make a genuine effort to find out what is valued by the employee or customer, and then they give more of it than was expected. Very often, lagniappe doesn't cost a dime.

By exceeding the expectation, these companies send a powerful message: "You are important." "I am genuinely concerned about you and your needs." "I will do whatever I can to make you satisfied." And every time, without fail, employees respond with reciprocal loyalty and a strong desire to give back a little more than what the job description requires. This is the cradle of truly great success.

NORDSTROM'S LAGNIAPPE

The documented tales of Nordstrom's Department Stores' outstanding customer service are legendary. At a customer's request, one shoe salesperson nailed a newly purchased shoe onto the customer's wooden foot. Another salesperson personally delivered a newly altered pair of pants to a customer's home on his way home from work. Michele Love, manager of the Skokie, Illinois store, even opened a mammography center in the store when a customer casually mentioned there wasn't one in the area. The center has been continually booked since it opened.

James Nordstrom ("Mr. Jim" as employees call him) is the Nordstrom family's crown prince and guardian of their philosophy of giving customer service that wins accolades both from customers and industry watch groups, and, most importantly, at the cash register. His message is ingrained into every store manager: "This is your own business. Do your own thing. Don't listen to us in Seattle [corporate headquarters]. Listen to your customer. We give you permission to take care of your customer."[1]

It is a philosophy that pays. In 1995, not a particularly great year for most department stores, Nordstrom's net margin was 4.5 percent, compared to 2 percent for the giant retailer Federated Department Stores and 2.7 percent average for the entire industry.

The principle of lagniappe permeates the entire Nordstrom operation. Because the company believes that a missing item is a missing sale and, worse, a disappointed customer, it carries inventories equal to $65 per square foot, twice as much as the industry average. The May stores carry about $40 per square foot; Federated less than $30. In shoes alone the store carries sizes 7 to 17EEEE—a size one employee describes as a virtual water ski.

Nordstrom stores are among the only retailers that still offer the services of the grand old department stores of years gone by. Shoppers may check packages at a concierge desk, enjoy an espresso at the coffee bar, or consult with a personal wardrobe specialist in the Personal Touch department. Live music flows from a grand piano that has become a Nordstrom signature piece. Comfortable chairs are generously dispersed among the merchandise for the foot-weary shopper's companion.

The lagniappe doesn't stop when it comes to employees,

either. In exchange for their personal commitment to customer service, sales employees are guaranteed base pay of between $5 and $11 an hour. With commissions ranging from
6.57 percent on apparel sales to around 13 percent on children's shoes, an above-average salesperson can gross $75,000
to $80,000 a year.

Not surprisingly, the employees return the lagniappe. According to a survey by *Women's Wear Daily*, the women's apparel trade magazine, Nordstrom was rated the best store for
sales personnel and service by 77 percent of the women sur-
veyed. Several years ago, when a small group of disgruntled
employees aired their differences with Nordstrom to the press,
the Seattle flagship store was besieged with protesters—
current Nordstrom employees who were protesting on their
own time in defense of their employer.

Patrick McCarthy is, without a doubt, the quintessential
Nordstrom salesperson. He sells men's tailored clothing in the
Seattle store. Now in his twenty-sixth year with the company,
McCarthy has been the top salesperson for fifteen years in a
row. With a personal client list of 6,000, he sells more than
$1.5 million worth of merchandise a year. Like most Nords-
trom salespersons, he stays abreast of all inventory and personally contacts clients when merchandise comes in that
matches the customer's taste and size. A slogan that used to
be posted on every Nordstrom cash register seems to sum it
up best: "Everybody has access to the same merchandise; the
difference is the people who sell the merchandise."[2]

THE POWER OF PERSONAL LAGNIAPPE

Effective lagniappe is more than a corporate slogan: It is a
personal philosophy of management. Each member of the organization must change in some small way before the whole
makes the turn. No small feat, this is the key to change—each
individual learning from observation that the practice of
lagniappe is the only way to succeed in the organization.

If morale is to change for the better, employees must have
the opportunity to learn from the example of their managers

that giving a little more to their jobs is worthwhile. This is an environment where employees want to give more, not one where they feel forced or manipulated into giving more. When this happens, the tremendous power of lagniappe is realized.

Lagniappe is as much a personal philosophy as it is a management tactic. When people give more than what is required to their job, they eventually learn that they get back more than they expected. Those who work with them are also willing to give more, creating a work environment that is geared for productivity and success.

No one gets much satisfaction from a job where they do only the minimum required. But when employees invest a little more time, energy, and thought than is required, the payback is satisfaction and contentment. The practice of personal lagniappe is the only way to improve organizational morale.

So powerful is personal lagniappe, it can sometimes survive in the most narcissistic of organizations. Some of the most creative employees learn from childhood that satisfaction only comes from going the extra mile. They lower their shoulders to the wheel and try to ignore the manipulative tactics that swirl around them daily. For them, the only reward for their labor comes from their personal satisfaction.

Once the power of lagniappe is released in an organization, it spreads contagiously. The extra that comes from going just a little farther than what is expected can make a significant difference for both company management and employees.

Lagniappe is the complete antithesis of corporate narcissism. It is the kernel of truth that is missing from the organization consumed with self-interest. The narcissistic practice of giving less may offer a brief respite from a downward slide, but will eventually only accelerate financial retreat.

Lagniappe is a living contradiction—a paradox—that may be difficult to accept when hard times are frightfully near. Consider the analogy of the novice downhill skier, who must learn the difficult lesson of leaning *into* her downward flight if she wants to control it. Pulling back may abruptly stop the free fall, but it will never allow her to achieve her goal of gracefully traversing the mountain.

Perhaps this is why the management of so many corporations have found the narcissistic culture so comforting. It soothes their fears by playing to their misguided instincts. When things are out of control, one's natural reaction is to stop, pull back, and start again. So it is for the executives of today's corporations. This knee-jerk counteraction may end the immediate danger, but it also robs the company of time and intellectual capital. The practice of lagniappe is the ultimate mastery of skill over thoughtless reaction. It is cardinal to the art of management.

Lagniappe strikes at the very heart of narcissism; it creates an organizational environment that is a reluctant host to the self-serving power schemes of the narcissist. If wisely practiced by top management and rewarded throughout the organization, it will make the difference between sustainable success and inevitable failure.

Notes

PREFACE

1. Alice Miller, *The Drama of the Gifted Child* (New York: Basic Books, 1981).

INTRODUCTION

1. "The Making of a Corporate Tough Guy," *Business Week,* January 15, 1996.
2. William Safire, "Beware of the New Socialism Under the Banner of 'Social Responsibility,'" *San Jose Mercury News,* February 27, 1996, p. 7B.
3. Ronald E. Seavoy, *The Origins of the American Business Corporation: 1784–1855* (Westport, Conn.: Greenwood Press, 1982), p. 237.
4. Matthew Josephson, *The Robber Barons* (New York: Harcourt, Brace & World, 1962).

CHAPTER ONE

1. M. M. Innes, trans., *Metamorphoses of Ovid* (Harmondsworth, England: Penguin Books, 1955), pp. 83–87.

CHAPTER THREE

1. Maryann Keller, *Rude Awakening* (New York: HarperCollins, 1989), p. 66.

2. John Z. De Lorean and J. Patrick Wright, *On a Clear Day You Can See General Motors* (New York: Avon, 1979), p. 47.

3. Howard S. Schwartz, *Narcissistic Process and Corporate Decay* (New York: New York University Press, 1990), p. 60.

CHAPTER FOUR

1. Jay Cocks, "The Updated Book of Jobs," *Time* (January 3, 1982), p. 25.

2. *Wall Street Journal* (August 1980).

3. Cocks, "The Updated Book of Jobs."

4. Jeffrey S. Young, *The Journey Is the Reward* (New York: Scott, Foresman and Company, 1987).

5. Ibid., p. 188.

6. *Business Week* (January 31, 1983), p. 70.

7. Various Steve Jobs references: Young, *The Journey Is the Reward*; Michael Mortiz, *The Little Kingdom* (New York: William Morrow & Company, 1984); "Playboy Interview: Steven Jobs," *Playboy* (February 1985).

8. Darell Huff and Irving Geis, *How to Lie With Statistics* (New York: W. W. Norton, 1954).

9. Beatrice Garcia, "At What Price Safety? Issue Isn't Just ValuJet's," *Miami Herald* (May 27, 1996).

10. Matthew Wald, "U.S. Says ValuJet Ignored DC-9 Defects," *New York Times* (June 20, 1996).

11. ValuJet Airlines, "Onward and Upward: Four Airline Guys, The Critter, Captain Valu and the Sage of ValuJet (An Uplifting Tale)" (1996).

12. Garcia, "At What Price Safety?"

13. Mark Maremont, "Blind Ambition: How the Pursuit of Results Got Out of Hand at Bausch & Lomb," *Business Week* (October 23, 1995).

CHAPTER FIVE

1. Lee Gomes, "High-Flying Oracle Set Itself Up for a Fall," *San Jose Mercury News* (September 8, 1990), p. 11D.

2. Ibid.
3. "Comeback of the Decade: Larry Ellison," *Success* (August 1995), p. 34.
4. Eyal Press, *Nation* (July 31, 1995), p. 126.
5. "Is Suharto Backtracking?" *Business Week* (April 8, 1996).
6. Katherine Mangan, "Businessman Asks Loyola University to Return $600,000 Donation," *Chronicle of Higher Education* (December 8, 1995), p. A30.
7. *New Orleans Times-Picayune* (January 28, 1996), p. A19.
8. Press, *Nation.*
9. Stewart Yerton, *New Orleans Times-Picayune* (January 28, 1996), p. A21.
10. Mangan, "Businessman Asks Loyola University."
11. Alfred Charles, "City Council Goes to Bat for Freeport, Moffett," *New Orleans Times-Picayune,* p. B1.
12. Katherine Mangan, *Chronicle of Higher Education* (January 5, 1996), p. A43.
13. Press, *Nation.*
14. Alexander Cockburn, *Nation* (August 12, 1996), p. 24.
15. "Gold Rush in New Guinea," *Business Week* (November 20, 1995).

CHAPTER SIX

1. Kim Cameron, "Downsizing, Quality and Performance," in *The Death and Life of the American Quality Movement,* Robert Cole, ed. (New York: Oxford University Press, 1995), p. 6.
2. David Kearns and David Nadler, *Prophets in the Dark: How Xerox Reinvented Itself and Beat Back the Japanese* (New York: HarperBusiness, 1992).

CHAPTER SEVEN

1. Elise Walton, "Generative Strategy," in *Discontinuous Change: Leading Organizational Transformation* (San Francisco: Jossey-Bass, 1995), p. 126.
2. Personal interview with author.

CHAPTER NINE

1. Jim Impoco, "Working for Mr. Clean Jeans: Levi's Leader Robert Haas Cares About Morals as Well as Making Money," *U.S. News & World Report* (August 2, 1993), p. 49.
2. Joanna Ramey, "Apparel's Ethics Dilemma," *Women's Wear Daily* (March 18, 1996), p. 10.
3. Ibid.
4. "Managing By Values: Is Levi Strauss's Approach Visionary—Or Flaky?" *Business Week* (August 1, 1994).
5. Ibid.
6. Impoco, "Working for Mr. Clean Jeans."
7. Thomas Ryan, "Levi's Creates Incentive Plan for Employees," *Women's Wear Daily*, p. 2.
8. Joan O.C. Hamilton, "Levi's Pot O' Gold," *Business Week* (June 24, 1996).
9. Ibid.
10. John Case, "Quality With Tears," *Inc.* (June 1992).
11. David Bollier, *Aiming Higher: Twenty-Five Stories of How Companies Prosper by Combining Sound Management and Social Vision* (New York: AMACOM, 1996).

EPILOGUE

1. Seth Lubove, "Don't Listen to the Boss, Listen to the Customer," *Forbes* (December 4, 1995), p. 45.
2. "Patrick McCarthy of Nordstrom," *Daily News Record* (March 28, 1996), p. 12.

Index

Aiming Higher (Bollier), 189
alienation, 28
Allen, Robert, 87
Allied-Signal, 87
Andersen Consulting, 133–134
Andreas, Dwayne, 86
Andreas, Michael D. "Mick," 86
anger
    of enablers, 70
    at manipulation by narcissists,
        40–42, 55–62, 65–66, 70,
        174–175
appearances, importance of, 14–
    18, 20–21, 115–125
Apple Computer, 92–102
Apple II, 94–99, 102
A & P supermarkets, 104
Archer Daniels Midland Co.
    (ADM), 85–86
Atkinson, Bill, 93–94
AT&T, 87

Bangladesh, 178–183
Bausch & Lomb, 106–110
Bennis, Warren, 88
Boeing Co., 87–88
Bollier, David, 189
bonuses, 107–110, 183
Bossidy, Lawrence, 87
Braccini, Cinde, 188
Braccini, Steve, 185–189
Bread and Roses labor strike,
    203

Buchanan, Pat, 205
Bureau of Labor Statistics
    (BLS), 89

Cameron, Kim, 131
Carnegie, Andrew, 4
Chan, Y. H., 109
change, resistance to, 80,
    175–176
charters, corporate, 3–4
China, 178
closed systems, 82–85
coaches, executive, 199–200
communication
    control of information in, 42–
        45, 115–125
    honesty in, 157–160, 182
    manipulation of feedback, 85–
        86, 116–125
    in meetings, 44–45, 83
    spin on setbacks, 42–43
    written, 43–44
compensation
    bonuses in, 107–110, 183
    corporate layoffs and, 89–90,
        128–129, 134–135, 205
    empire building and, 48
    executive stock options in,
        87–88
    gaps in growth and decline of,
        87–88, 205
    greed and, 48, 86–90
    self-worth and, 194

competitiveness
  handling, 167–168
  in narcissism, 91–101, 106,
    165, 166–168
Concept of a Corporation, The
    (Drucker), 85
conflict
  avoiding, 169–170
  handling, 171
  "head-on collisions," 63–64
  in narcissism, 63–64, 165,
    168–171
  wasting energy in, 125
consultants, 133–135
control
  of communications, 42–45,
    115–125
  of decision making, 45–48,
    81–82, 198
  see also power
Coopers & Lybrand, 134
core competencies, 143–160
  hiring and promotion in,
    146–148
  honest communication and,
    157–160, 182
  identifying, 143–146
  performance appraisal and,
    156–157
  training and, 148–156
Corporate Executions (Downs),
    89
corporate narcissists, 31–73
  advantages of working for, 63
  "checking out" and, 66
  competitiveness of, 91–101,
    106, 165, 166–168
  compliance with, 64–65,
    198–199
  conflict and, 63–64, 165,
    168–171
  control of communications by,
    42–45, 115–125

control of decision making by,
    45–48, 81–82, 198
  costs of, 32–35, 101–102
  empire building by, 48–49, 79,
    198–199
  enablers of, 66–73
  futility of changing, 163–164
  incompatibility of motivations
    and, 165, 171–174
  lack of self-confidence, 14,
    19–20, 48, 67–68, 164, 175,
    194–195, 197
  loyalty to company of, 35–36
  manipulation of others by, 21–
    22, 37–42, 55–62, 85–86,
    148, 197–198
  modern Narcissus and, 14–18
  need for power, 36–37, 48,
    67–68, 69, 81–82, 164, 169,
    170, 198
  need for visibility, 49–51, 63,
    164, 166, 168, 198
  passing of blame by, 51–54
  personal use of resources by,
    36
  pseudo-creativity of, 54–55
  resistance to change by, 80,
    175–176
  softening style of, 199–201
  top management and,
    161–163
  workaholism of, 35, 186
  working with, 55–73, 161–176
corporate parentalism, 2, 68
corporation
  charter of, 3–4
  as dangerous entity, 4
  history of American, 3–5
  mission of, *see* mission, corpo-
    rate
Couch, John, 96–97
cross-functional teams, 144–
    146, 182

CSC/Index, Inc., 134
Cubbage, Paul, 114
Cunningham, William, 122
curve balls, 47–48
customer focus, 155–156, 185–
    189, 206–208
Cypress Semiconductor, 2

Daniell, Robert, 87
Dataquest, 114
Davis, Tommye Jo, 182
decision making
    control of, 45–48, 81–82, 198
    curve balls and, 47–48
    narcissistic trust and, 46–47
De Lorean, John, 82–83
Delta Consulting, 134–135
dependency needs, 69–70,
    80–81
downsizing, 89–90, 128–129,
    134–135, 205
Drucker, Peter, 85
Dunlap, Albert, 3

Egan, Thomas, 122
Ellison, Larry, 113–115
empathy, lack of, 20, 21–22, 37,
    39–40
enablers, 66–73
    burnout of, 70–73
    characteristics of, 66–69
    links to narcissists, 67, 69–70
environmental protection,
    116–125
ethical issues:
    sweatshop labor, 178–183
    value-centered management,
    177–185
ethics, lapses in, 111–115
executive coaches, 199–200
executive stock options, 87–88
extrinsic motivation, 171–174

Federal Aviation Administration
    (FAA), 105–106
feedback, manipulation of, 85–
    86, 116–125
Feuerstein, Aaron, 203–204
financial reporting, 106–110,
    114–115
Ford, Henry, 5
Freeport-MacMorRan case
    study, 116–125
future, focus on, 196–197

Garcia, Beatrice, 106
General Motors, 82–83, 85
Gill, Dan, 107–110
Glass, David, 179
greed
    compensation and, 48, 86–90
    competitiveness and, 168
    see also legal issues

Haas, Robert, 178, 181, 183
Haas School of Business, 88
Hafild, Emily, 121
Hammer, Michael, 135–136
Hawkins, Trip, 96
Hellman, F. Warren, 181
herd mentality, 127–136
    layoffs and, 128–129
    power and, 130–135
    quality and, 131–132,
    135–136
hiring practices, 146–148
honesty, 157–160, 182
How to Lie With Statistics
    (Huff), 103–104
Huff, Darrell, 103–104
human rights violations, 116–
    125, 178–183

IBM, 97, 113
identity, corporate, 139–146

immersion management, 81–82
incompatibility, 165, 171–174
    handling, 173–174
    locus of motivation and,
        171–174
Indonesia, 116–125
influence-peddling, 5
innovation
    pseudo-creativity versus,
        54–55
    requirements of, 206
intrinsic motivation, 171–174
Irvin, John, 151
isolation, 28

Jobs, Steve, 92–102
Josephson, Matthew, 4

Kabuki, Michael, 179
Kearns, David, 134–135
Keller, Maryann, 82–83
Kelly, George, 196

lagniappe, 204–210
    business growth and, 206
    nature of, 204–206
    of Nordstrom Department
        Stores, 206–208
    personal, 208–210
Landau, Robert, 188–189
layoffs, 89–90, 128–129, 134–
    135, 205
legal issues:
    environmental protection,
        116–125
    financial reporting, 106–110,
        114–115
    human rights violations, 116–
        125, 178–183
    price fixing, 85–86
    safety regulations, 85,
        104–106

Levine, David, 88
Levi Strauss, 177–185
Lisa computer, 92–102
lobbying, 5
locus of motivation, 165,
    171–174
    incompatibility and, 172–173
    nature of, 171–172
Love, Michele, 207
loyalty, to company, 35–36

Macintosh computer, 97–102
Malcolm Baldrige Award, 131
Malden Mills, 203–204
management consultants,
    133–135
management seminars, 201
manipulation
    of feedback, 85–86, 116–125
    in narcissism, 21–22, 37–42,
        55–62, 85–86, 148,
        197–198
    resentment caused by, 40–42,
        55–62, 65–66, 70, 174–175
Marsh, Bruce, 121
Marvyn's Department Store,
    148–156
Massachusetts Bay Company, 3
McCarthy, Patrick, 208
McDermott, Thomas, 107
McKinney, James, 88
McKinsey & Co., 134
media, values-centered manage-
    ment and, 106, 183–185,
    208
meetings, narcissists controlling,
    44–45, 83
Millstein, Alan G., 184
mission, corporate
    core competencies in,
        143–160
    early charters and, 3–4

loss of, 6, 78–79
organizational self-awareness
    and, 139–146
for stakeholders versus stock-
    holders, 2–3, 5, 183
values-centered management
    and, 177–183
mistakes, 51–54
    admitting, 195–196
    avoiding truth and, 157–160
    diverting blame for, 52–53
    scapegoating and, 53–54, 69,
        113, 133
Moffett, Jim Bob, 120, 124
Morgan, J. Pierpont, 4
motivation, compatibility of,
    165, 171–174

Nader, Ralph, 85
Nadler, David, 134–135
narcissism
    appearances and, 14–18, 20–
        21, 115–125
    awareness of personal,
        193–199
    changing, 163–164
    costs of, 32–35, 101–102
    developmental origins of,
        18–20
    individual, *see* corporate nar-
        cissists
    isolation and alienation in, 28
    lack of empathy in, 20, 21–22,
        37, 39–40
    lack of self-confidence in, 14,
        19–20, 48, 67–68, 164, 175,
        194–195, 197
    lack of trust and, 28, 40–42
    loyalty to company in, 35–36
    manipulation of others and,
        21–22, 37–42, 55–62, 85–
        86, 148, 197–198

modern Narcissus, 14–18
myth of Narcissus, 13–14
nature of, 12–14, 193–199
need for power in, 36–37, 48,
    67–68, 69, 81–82, 164, 169,
    170, 198
need for validation in, 17–18,
    19, 28
organizational, *see* organiza-
    tional narcissism
pain of, 22–27
as personal facade, 27–29, 67
personal tendencies toward,
    193–199
personal use of resources in,
    36
vicious cycle of, 22, 26–27
workaholism in, 35, 186
Narcissus, 13–14
Nordstrom, James, 207
Nordstrom Department Stores,
    206–208

Oracle Systems Corp., 113–115
organizational narcissism,
    77–136
    appearances and, 115-125
    centralized power in, 81–82
    closed systems in, 82–85
    compulsion to win in, 110
    corporate scoreboards in,
        102–106
    costs of, 101–102
    denial of reality in, 106–110,
        196–197
    derailing of business move-
        ments in, 135–136
    ethical issues and, 111–115,
        177–185
    fighting, 139–160, 189–190
    focus on profits in, 2, 3, 78,
        103–106, 110, 111–125

organizational narcissism
    (*continued*)
  herd mentality and, 127–136
  idolized leaders in, 80–81
  layoffs and, 89–90, 128–129,
    134–135, 205
  legal issues concerning, *see*
    legal issues
  loss of mission in, 6, 78–79
  management consultants and,
    133–135
  manipulation of feedback in,
    85–86, 116–125
  organizational structure and,
    79–80, 144–146
  passion for greed in, 48,
    86–90
  positive intentions in,
    115–125
  resistance to change in, 80,
    175–176
  rules of, 77–78
  sacrifice of quality in, 131–
    132, 134–135
  spread of, 11–12, 77–78
  techniques for reducing, 199–
    201, 204–210
  top management and,
    161–163
  values-centered management
    versus, 177–191, 204–210
  working with, 55–73, 161–176
organizational structure, 79–80,
    144–146
Overseas Private Investment
    Corporation (OPIC),
    119–120
Ovid, on Narcissus, 13–14

performance appraisal, 36, 156–
    157, 182, 200–201
Pfeffer, Jeffrey, 88

Plymouth Company, 3
power
  centralized, 81–82
  herd mentality and, 130–135
  need for, 36–37, 48, 67–68,
    69, 81–82, 164, 169, 170,
    198
  see also control
present, focus on, 196–197
price fixing, 85–86
Pro Fasteners Inc. (PFI),
    185–189
profit
  environmental issues and,
    116–125
  herd mentality and, 127–136
  layoffs and, 89–90, 128–129,
    134–135, 205
  safety issues and, 85, 104–106
  as Ultimate Corporate Man-
    date, 2, 3, 78, 103–106,
    110, 111–125
promotion practices, 146–148
Prophets in the Dark (Kearns
    and Nadler), 134–135
pseudo-creativity, 54–55
purists, *see* shareholder-purists

quality movement
  continuous-improvement pro-
    grams of, 186–189
  hijacking of, 135–136
  sacrifice of quality and, 131–
    132, 134–135

Raskin, Jeff, 95
Reengineering the Corporation
    (Hammer), 135–136
resentment, of manipulation,
    40–42, 55–62, 65–66, 70,
    174–175
resignation, 174

resistance
  to change, 80, 175–176
  to organizational narcissism, 139–160, 189–190
restructuring, 89–90, 128–129, 134–135, 205
return on investment, 104
  in corporate mission, 2–3
  in training, 151–152
reverse psychology, 37–38
Robber Barons, The (Josephson), 4
Robinette, Garland, 120–121
Rocky, Robert D., 182
Rodgers, T. J., 2
Rogers, Carl, 19
Roosevelt, Theodore, 4
Rothmueller, Ken, 94, 95
Rude Awakening (Keller), 82–83

safety, 85, 104–106
Safire, William, on stakeholders as socialists, 3
sales targets, 106–110, 113–115
Salyer, Sandy, 151
scapegoating, 53–54, 69, 113, 133
Schultz, Howard, 190
scoreboards, corporate, 102–106
Securities and Exchange Commission (SEC), 109–110, 114–115
self-awareness
  organizational, 139–146
  personal, 163, 164–165, 176, 186, 193–199
self-confidence, lack of, 14, 19–20, 48, 67–68, 164, 175, 194–195, 197
seminars, management, 201
setbacks, disguising, 42–43

shareholder-purists
  in the decade of the 1980s, 5–6
  as narcissists, 6–7
  return on investment and, 2–3, 104, 151–152
  robber barons as, 4
  stakeholders versus, 2–3, 5, 183
Shrontz, Frank, 87–88
situational interviews, 147–148
Smith, Roger, 82–83
socialism, 2, 3
stakeholders
  defined, 2
  focus on, 5
  history of American corporation and, 3–5
  shareholder-purists versus, 2–3, 5, 183
Starbucks Coffee Company, 189–190
stock market collapse, 4–5
stock options, 87–88
Sunbeam, 3
surrogate parent, 69
surveys, 360° performance, 157, 182, 200–201

teams
  competitiveness and, 168
  cross-functional, 144–146, 182
  values-centered management and, 182
360° performance reviews, 157, 182, 200–201
top management, 161–163
total quality movement, 131–132, 134–135, 186–189
training, 148–156, 201

trust
    lack of, 28, 40–42
    manipulation and, 40–42
    narcissistic, 46–47
    nature of, 46
trust-busting, 4
truth, honesty in communica-
    tion and, 157–160, 182

unconditional positive regard,
    19–20
United Technologies, 87
University of Southern Califor-
    nia, 88
Unsafe at Any Speed (Nader), 85

validation, need for, 17–18, 19,
    28
values-centered management,
    177–191
    lagniappe in, 204–210
    at Levi Strauss, 177–185

at Pro Fasteners Inc. (PFI),
    185–189
at Starbucks Coffee Company,
    189–190
ValuJet, 104–106
Vanderbilt, Cornelius, 4
visibility, need for, 49–51, 63,
    164, 166, 168, 198

Wal-Mart, 179
Walton, Elise, 139
Waltrip, William, 110
Whitacre, Mark, 85–86
"win-win" situations, 91
Wood, William, 203
workaholism, 35, 186
Wozniak, Steve, 94
written communication, 43–
    44

Xerox, 134–135

Yates, Carolyn, 155